The Subcommittee on the Catechism, United States Conference of Catholic Bishops, has found this catechetical series, copyright 2011, to be in conformity with the *Catechism of the Catholic Church.*

Photo Credits

Cover Photography: Corbis/amanaimages/UVimages: *starry night sky*; Neal Farris: *girl*; Getty Images/Photodisc/C Squared Studios: *bible*; Getty Images/Photonica/Silvia Otte: *Brooklyn Bridge*; Ken Karp: *boy*. Interior: Alamy/Mike Goldwater: 24; Image Source Pink: 244 *bottom right*; Israel Images/Hanan Isachar: 32; JUPITERIMAGES/Creatas: 216; Linda Kennedy: 209 *bottom*; Kolvenbach: 97; Robert Mayne USA: 170. Art Resource, NY: 67; Scala: 88, 90, 182, 225 *top*. Jane Bernard: 65, 116 *bottom*, 185 *right*, 214 *bottom*. The Bridgeman Art Library/Philip Mould Ltd, London/Private Collection/Portrait of Sir Thomas More (1478–1535) (panel), Holbein, Hans the Younger (1497/8–1543) (after): 49. Karen Callaway: 7, 53, 54, 65, 73 *right*, 101, 108 *bottom left*, 109 *bottom right*, 110, 116 *top*, 136, 185, 214 *top*, 241 *bottom*. Clipart.com: 244 *top left*. Corbis/Arte & Immagini srl: 62; Rolf Bruderer: 17 *top right*, 55 *right*; Laura Dwight: 185 *center right*, 241 *center*; Julie Houck: 189; Charles & Josette Lenars: 118; Lawrence Manning: 141; Mug Shots: 55 *left*; Alan Shein Photography: 27 *background*; Leif Skoogfors: 33; Ted Spiegel: 100; Visions of America/Joseph Sohm: 158. The Crosiers/Gene Plaisted, OSC: 23, 41, 59 *bottom right*, 64, 113 *top*, 174. Digital Stock Corporation: 22. Courtesy of famvin.org: 169. Neal Farris: 8, 19, 27 *bottom*, 36, 37, 39 *top*, 56, 73 *center left*, 74, 75, 91 *bottom*, 99, 121, 129 *left*, 129 *center*, 147, 156, 163, 166–167, 177, 190, 191, 196 *bottom*, 198–199, 203, 211, 215, 219. Fundación Teresa de Los Andes: 209 *top*. Getty Images/AFP/Vicenzo Pinto: 225 *bottom*; Digital Vision/Flying Colours Ltd: 150 *left*; The Image Bank/Ghislain & Marie David de Lossy: 51; The Image Bank/Brooklyn Productions: 133; The Image Bank/Kaz Mori: 107 *background*; Photodisc/Tony Anderson: 150 *right*; Photodisc/C Squared Studios: 147 *bottom*; Photodisc/Kevin Peterson: 244 *bottom center*; Photodisc/StockTrek: 91 *background*; Photodisc/SW Productions: 220; Photographer's Choice/Patti McConville: 134; Riser/Jon Riley: 132; Stockbyte: 148 *center*, 148 *center left*, 148 *center right*, 148 *bottom left*, 149 *center*, 243; Stone/Brad Hitz: 195; Stone/Stuart Westmoreland: 17 *center left*, 47, 241 *top*; Stone/Zig Kaluzny–Charles Thatcher: 212 *top*. Grant Heilman Photography, Inc./Larry Lefever: 121 *background*. Jupiter Images/liquidlibrary: 168 *right*; Pixland: 244 *bottom left*; Wood River Gallery: 221. Ken Karp: 10, 11, 12, 13, 14, 16 *top*, 35, 43, 92, 107, 115, 122, 123, 124, 126, 131, 139, 148 *top left*, 148 *top right*, 148 *bottom right*, 149 *top*, 149 *bottom*, 171, 187, 227. Robert Lentz, OFM, St. Isidore and St. Maria, © 2010, Courtesy of Trinity Stores, www.trinitystores.com, (800) 699 4482: 201. Portrait of St. Alphonsus Liguori by G. A. Lomuscio, copyright © 1994 Redemptorist Fathers/Liguori Publications, www.liguori.org. All rights reserved. Used by permission: 57. Greg Lord: 84–85, 111. Marquette University: 25. Ronald Molino: 193. Robert Mullen: 145. Office Central de Lisieux: 137. Douglas Peebles: 144. PhotoEdit, Inc./Jeff Greenberg: 135 *right*. Photolibrary/Sandra Baker: 135 *left*; Frank Conaway: 152 *bottom*; Mark Polott: 83; Miro Vintoniv: 80; Zephyr Picture: 129 *right*. Punchstock/Digital Vision: 208; Image Source: 96. Saint Joseph's Abbey, Spencer, MA: 15, 89. The Society of Saint Vincent de Paul: 168 *left*. Chris Sheridan: 108–109. Andrew Sroka: 172. SuperStock/Koji Kitagawa: 19 *background*. Jim Whitmer Photography: 152. W.P. Wittman Ltd: 59 *top right*, 105, 113 *bottom*, 120, 176, 178, 179 *top*, 179 *bottom*, 180, 212 *bottom right*, 217, 230, 249.

Illustrator Credits

Series Patterned Background: Evan Polenghi. Bassino & Guy: 96, 104. 201. Teresa Berasi: 144. Nan Brooks: 190–191. Janet Broxon: 73 *left*. Penny Carter: 156–157, 160. Bob Dombrowski: 165. Jeff Fitz-Maurice: 212–213. Annie Gusman: 81. Nick Harris: 76–77. Mary Haverfield: 206–207. Lydia Hess: 92, 93. Jacey: 17 *middle*, 45, 86–87. W. B. Johnston: 102–103, 131, 203, 214–215. Ken Joudrey: 35. Jared Lee: 48. Dave Klug: 153, 200. Robert LoGrippo: 17 *left*. David McGlynn: 55. Frank Ordaz: vi, 17 *right*, 20–21, 28–29, 30–31, 38, 44, 46, 47, 52, 60 *inset*, 73 *right*, 78–79, 129 *right*, 164, 185, 188–189, 204–206, 229, 232, 241. Leah Palmer Preiss: 73 *middle*, 94, 95. Donna Perrone: 129 *left*, 140. Gary Phillips: 57, 142–143. Mike Radencich: 100–101. Zina Saunders: 161, 242. J. W. Stewart: 222–223. Amanda Warren: 59–70, 171–182, 227–232, 242 *top*. Liz Wheaton: 134–135. Amy Wummer: 40, 115–126, 137, 169. 192 *top*. Dirk Wunderlich: 36–37. Heidi Younger: 186, 192 *bottom*, 217.

The Sadlier *We Believe* Program was drawn from the wisdom of the community. It was developed by nationally recognized experts in catechesis, curriculum, and child development. These teachers of the faith and practitioners helped us to frame every lesson to be age-appropriate and appealing. In addition, a team including respected catechetical, liturgical, pastoral, and theological experts shared their insights and inspired the development of the program.

Contributors to the inspiration and development are:

Dr. Gerard F. Baumbach
Director, Center for Catechetical Initiatives
Concurrent Professor of Theology
University of Notre Dame
Notre Dame, Indiana

Carole M. Eipers, D.Min.
Vice President, Executive Director
    of Catechetics
William H. Sadlier, Inc.

Catechetical and Liturgical Consultants

Patricia Andrews
Director of Religious Education
Our Lady of Lourdes Church,
Slidell, LA

Reverend Monsignor John F. Barry, P.A.
Pastor, American Martyrs Parish
Manhattan Beach, CA

Mary Jo Tully
Chancellor, Archdiocese of Portland

Reverend Monsignor John M. Unger
Deputy Superintendent for Catechesis
    and Evangelization
Archdiocese of St. Louis

Curriculum and Child Development Consultants

Brother Robert R. Bimonte, FSC
Executive Director
NCEA Department of Elementary Schools

Sr. Carol Cimino, SSJ, Ed.D.
National Consultant
William H. Sadlier

Gini Shimabukuro, Ed.D.
Associate Professor
Catholic Educational Leadership Program
School of Education
University of San Francisco

Catholic Social Teaching Consultants

John Carr
Executive Director
Department of Justice, Peace,
    and Human Development
United States Conference of Catholic Bishops
Washington, D.C.

Joan Rosenhauer
Associate Director
Department of Justice, Peace,
    and Human Development
United States Conference of Catholic Bishops
Washington, D.C.

Inculturation Consultants

Allan Figueroa Deck, S.J., Ph.D., S.T.D.
Executive Director
Secretariat of Cultural Diversity in the Church
United States Conference of Catholic Bishops
Washington, D.C.

Kirk P. Gaddy, Ed.D.
Educational Consultant
Baltimore, MD

Reverend Nguyễn Việt Hưng
Vietnamese Catechetical Committee

Dulce M. Jiménez-Abreu
Director of Bilingual Programs
William H. Sadlier, Inc.

Sadlier

We Believe™

God's Law
Guides Us

WITH PROJECT DISCIPLE
Pray
Learn
Celebrate
Share
Choose
Live

Grade Four

Sadlier

Nihil Obstat
Monsignor Michael F. Hull, S.T.D.
Censor Librorum

Imprimatur
✠ Most Reverend Dennis J. Sullivan, D.D.
Vicar General of the Archdiocese of New York
January 27, 2010

The *Nihil Obstat* and *Imprimatur* are official declaration that these books are free of doctrinal or moral error. No implications contained therein that those who have granted the *Nihil Obstat* and *Imprimatur* agree with the content, opinion or statements expressed.

Acknowledgments

Excerpts from the English translation of *The Roman Missal*, © 2010, International Committee on English in the Liturgy, Inc. All rights reserved.

Excerpts from the English translation of the *Catechism of the Catholic Church* for the United States of America, copyright © 1994, United States Catholic Conference, Inc.—Libreria Editrice Vaticana. English translation of the *Catechism of the Catholic Church: Modifications from the Editio Typica* copyright © 1997, United States Catholic Conference, Inc.—Libreria Editrice Vaticana. Used with permission.

Scripture excerpts are taken from the *New American Bible with Revised New Testament and Psalms* Copyright © 1991, 1986, 1970, Confraternity of Christian Doctrine, Inc., Washington, D.C. Used with permission. All rights reserved. No part of the *New American Bible* may be reproduced by any means without permission in writing from the copyright owner.

Excerpts from the English translation of *Lectionary for Mass* © 1969, 1981, 1997, International Committee on English in the Liturgy, Inc. (ICEL); excerpts from the English translation of the *Rite of Penance* © 1974, ICEL; excerpts from the English translation of *A Book of Prayers* © 1982, ICEL. All rights reserved.

Excerpts from *Catholic Household Blessings and Prayers* Copyright © 1988 United States Catholic Conference, Inc., Washington, D.C. Used with permission. All rights reserved.

Excerpt from the prayer "God be in my head" from *The Oxford Book of Prayers* © 1985, Oxford University Press, Oxford, UK.

English translation of the Our Father, Glory to the Father, Apostles' Creed, *Gloria in Excelsis* and *Sanctus / Benedictus* by the International Consultation on English Texts. (ICET)

"We Believe, We Believe in God," © 1979, North American Liturgy Resources (NALR), 5536 NE Hassalo, Portland, OR 97213. All rights reserved. Used with permission. "Blest Are They," David Haas. Text: The Beatitudes. Text and music: © 1985, G.I.A. Publications, Inc. All rights reserved. Used with permission. "Come, Follow Me," © 1992, Barbara Bridge. Published by OCP Publications, 5536 NE Hassalo, Portland, OR 97213. All rights reserved. Used with permission. "Prayer of St. Francis," dedicated to Mrs. Frances Tracy. © 1967, OCP Publications, 5536 NE Hassalo, Portland, OR 97213. All rights reserved. Used with permission. "Lord, I Lift Your Name on High," Rick Founds. © 1989, 1999, MARANATHA PRAISE, INC. (Administered by THE COPYRIGHT COMPANY, Nashville, TN.) All rights reserved. International copyright secured. "Open Our Hearts," © 1989, Christopher Walker. Published by OCP Publications, 5536 NE Hassalo, Portland, OR 97213. All rights reserved. Used with permission. "Come to the Feast (Ven al Banquete)," © 1994, Bob Hurd and Pia Moriarty. Published by OCP Publications, 5536 NE Hassalo, Portland, OR 97213. All rights reserved. Used with permission. "Somos el Cuerpo de Cristo," © 1994, Jaime Cortez. Published by OCP Publications. All rights reserved. Used with permission. "Praise Him with Cymbals," © 1993, Janet Vogt. Published by OCP Publications, 5536 NE Hassalo, Portland, OR 97213. All rights reserved. Used with permission. "We Are the Family," Ray Repp. © 1979, K & R Music Publishing. From the recording *Sunrise, In the Dead of Winter*. All rights reserved. Used with permission. "You Are Near," © 1971, 1974, Daniel L. Schutte. Administered by New Dawn Music, 5536 NE Hassalo, Portland, OR 97213. All rights reserved. Used with permission. "I Am Special," © 1999, Bernadette Farrell. Published by OCP Publications, 5536 NE Hassalo, Portland, OR 97213. All rights reserved. Used with permission. "Though We Are Many / Make Us a Sign," © 1999, Bernadette Farrell. Published by OCP Publications, 5536 NE Hassalo, Portland, OR 97213. All rights reserved. Used with permission. "New Heart and New Spirit," © 1992, John Schiavone. Published by OCP Publications, 5536 NE Hassalo, Portland, OR 97213. All rights reserved. Used with permission. "We Are Yours, O Lord," © 1996, Janet Vogt. Published by OCP Publications, 5536 NE Hassalo, Portland, OR 97213. All rights reserved. Used with permission. "Lord, You Have Come (Pescador de Hombres)," Spanish text and music © 1979, Cesáreo Gabaráin. English translation by Robert C. Trupia, © 1987 by OCP Publications, 5536 NE Hassalo, Portland, OR 97213. All rights reserved. Used with permission. "You Call Us to Live," © 1990, Christopher Walker. Published by OCP Publications, 5536 NE Hassalo, Portland, OR 97213. All rights reserved. Used with permission. "Send Us Your Spirit," © 1988, 1989, 1990, Christopher Walker. Published by OCP Publications, 5536 NE Hassalo, Portland, OR 97213. All rights reserved. Used with permission.

William H. Sadlier, Inc.
9 Pine Street
New York, NY 10005-1002

ISBN: 978-0-8215-6404-2
456789 WEBC 15 14 13 12 11

Scriptural Consultant

Reverend Donald Senior, CP, Ph.D., S.T.D.
Member, Pontifical Biblical Commission
President, The Catholic Theological Union
Chicago, IL

Theological Consultants

Most Reverend Edward K. Braxton, Ph.D., S.T.D.
Official Theological Consultant
Bishop of Belleville, IL

Norman F. Josaitis, S.T.D.
Theological Consultant

Reverend Joseph A. Komonchak, Ph.D.
Professor, School of Theology and Religious Studies
The Catholic University of America

Most Reverend Richard J. Malone, Th.D.
Bishop of Portland, ME

Sister Maureen Sullivan, OP, Ph.D.
Associate Professor
St. Anselm College
Manchester, NH

Mariology Consultant

Sister M. Jean Frisk, ISSM, S.T.L.
International Marian Research Institute
Dayton, OH

Media/Technology Consultants

Sister Judith Dieterle, SSL
Past President, National Association of
Catechetical Media Professionals

Sister Jane Keegan, RDC
Technology Consultant

Michael Ferejohn
Director of Electronic Media
William H. Sadlier, Inc.

Robert T. Carson
Electronic Media Design Director
William H. Sadlier, Inc.

Erik Bowie
Electronic Media Production Manager
William H. Sadlier, Inc.

Writing/Development Team

Rosemary K. Calicchio
Vice President, Publications

Blake Bergen
Editorial Director

Melissa D. Gibbons
Director of Research and
Development

Maureen Gallo
Senior Editor, Project Director

Joanne McDonald
Senior Editor

Christian Garcia
Contributing Writer

MaryAnn Trevaskiss
Supervising Editor

Kathy Hendricks
Contributing Writer

William M. Ippolito
Executive Consultant

Allison Johnston
Senior Editor

Margherita Rotondi
Editorial Assistant

Sadlier Consulting Team

Michaela Burke Barry
Director of Consultant Services

Judith A. Devine
National Sales Consultant

Kenneth Doran
National Religion Consultant

Saundra Kennedy, Ed.D.
National Religion Consultant

Victor Valenzuela
National Religion Consultant

Publishing Operations Team

Deborah Jones
Vice President,
Publishing Operations

Vince Gallo
Creative Director

Francesca O'Malley
Associate Art Director

Jim Saylor
Photography Manager

Design/Photo Staff
Andrea Brown, Kevin Butler,
Debrah Kaiser, Susan Ligertwood,
Cesar Llacuna, Bob Schatz

Production Staff
Diane Ali, Monica Bernier,
Barbara Brown, Brent Burket,
Robin D'Amato, Stephen Flanagan,
Joyce Gaskin, Cheryl Golding,
Maria Jimenez, Joe Justus,
Vincent McDonough, Yolanda
Miley, Maureen Morgan, Jovito
Pagkalinawan, Monica Reece,
Julie Riley, Martin Smith

We are grateful to our loyal *We Believe* users whose insights and suggestions have inspired **PROJECT DISCIPLE**—the premier faith formation tool built on the six tasks of catechesis.

Contents

SEASONAL CHAPTERS

UNIT 3

The Commandments Help Us to Love Others

SEASONAL CHAPTERS

UNIT 4

We Are Called to Holiness............185

PROJECT DISCIPLE RESOURCES

We Believe

The *We Believe* program will help us to

learn

celebrate

share

and

live our Catholic faith.

We will read about:

Saint Alphonsus Liguori
Saint Augustine
Pope Benedict XVI
Saint Brigid
Saint Charles Lwanga and the Martyrs of Uganda
Dorothy Day
Saint Edith Stein
Saint Francis of Assisi
Frédéric Ozanam
Isaiah the Prophet
Saint Isidore
Saint John
Saint John the Baptist
Saint John of the Cross
Blessed John XXIII
Blessed Pope John Paul II
Saint John Vianney
Saint Joseph
Saint Josephine Bakhita
Saint Juan Diego

Blessed Kateri Tekakwitha
Saint Katharine Drexel
Saint Louise de Marillac
Blessed Louis and Zélie Martin
Saint Luke
Saint Maria
Saint Mark
Saint Matthew
Saint Monica
Oscar Romero
Our Lady of Guadalupe
Saint Paschal Baylon
Saint Paul
Saint Peter
Saint Peter Claver
Saint Rose Philippine Duchesne
Saint Teresa de los Andes
Saint Thérèse of the Child Jesus
Saint Thomas More
Saint Vincent de Paul

Together, let us grow as a community of faith.

Welcome!

> When we see **We Gather** we come together as a class.

WE GATHER

✝ **Leader:** Welcome, everyone, to Grade 4 *We Believe*. As we begin each chapter, we gather in prayer. We pray to God together. Sometimes, we will read from Scripture; other times we will say the prayers of the Church or sing a song of thanks and praise to God.

Today, let us sing the *We Believe* song!

♫ We Believe, We Believe in God

Refrain:

> We believe in God;
> We believe, we believe in Jesus;
> We believe in the Spirit who gives us life.
> We believe, we believe in God.
>
> We believe in the Holy Spirit,
> Who renews the face of the earth.
> We believe we are part of a living Church,
> And forever we will live with God.
>
> (Refrain)

We also focus on life.

 means it's time to

think about
talk about
act out
draw about
write about

Life

at school
at home
in our parish
in our world
in our neighborhood

Talk about your life right now. What groups, teams, or clubs do you belong to?

Why do you like being a part of these groups?

What does belonging to these groups tell other people about you?

Each day we learn more about God.

WE BELIEVE

We learn about:

- the Blessed Trinity—God the Father, God the Son, and God the Holy Spirit
- Jesus, the Son of God who became one of us
- the Church and its history and teachings
- the Mass and the sacraments
- our call to be a disciple of Jesus.

When we see **We Believe** we learn more about our Catholic faith.

UNIT 1 Growing in Jesus Christ
Jesus said, "I am the way and the truth and the life." (John 14:6)

UNIT 2 The Commandments Help Us to Love God
"LORD, teach me the way of your laws;
  I shall observe them with care." (Psalm 119:33)

UNIT 3 The Commandments Help Us to Love Others
"You shall love your neighbor as yourself." (Matthew 22:39)

UNIT 4 We Are Called to Holiness
"Do this in remembrance of me." (1 Corinthians 11:24)

A major theme in your *We Believe* textbook this year is learning more about the Ten Commandments. Your book is divided into four units.

Watch for these special signs:

Whenever we see ✝ we make the Sign of the Cross. We pray and begin our lesson.

📖 is an open Bible. When we see it, or a reference like this (John 13:34), we hear the Word of God. We hear about God and his people. We hear about Jesus and the Holy Spirit.

When we see 🏃 we do an activity. We might:

• talk together

• write a story

• draw a picture

• act out a story or situation

• imagine ourselves doing something

• sing a song together, or make up one

• work together on a special project.

There are all kinds of activities! We might see 🏃 in any part of our lesson. Be on the lookout!

Can you guess what 🎵 means? That's right, it means it is time to sing, or listen to music! We sing songs we know, make up our own, and sing along with those in our *We Believe* music program.

When we see **Key Words** we review the meanings of important words we have learned in the lesson.

As Catholics...

Here we discover something special about our faith. We reflect on what we have discovered and try to make it a part of our life. Don't forget to read it!

WE RESPOND

We can respond by:

- thinking about ways our faith affects the things we say and do

- sharing our thoughts and feelings

- praying to God.

Then in our home, neighborhood, school, parish, and world, we say and do the things that show love for God and others.

> When we see **We Respond** we reflect and act on what we have learned about God and our Catholic faith.

> We are so happy you are with us!

Draw yourself doing something that shows you are a disciple of Jesus Christ.

Show What you Know

We "show what we know" about each chapter's content. A disciple is always learning more about his or her faith.

More to Explore

We learn more about ways disciples are living out their faith.

Pray Today

We make time to talk and listen to God.

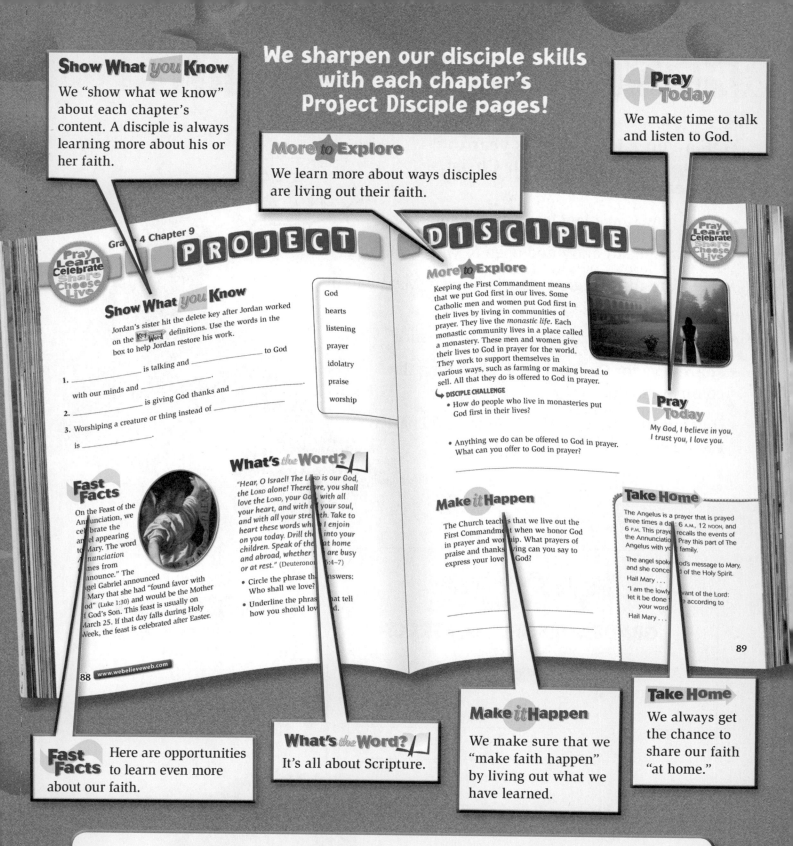

Grade 4 Chapter 9

PROJECT DISCIPLE

Show What you Know

Jordan's sister hit the delete key after Jordan worked on the Key Word definitions. Use the words in the box to help Jordan restore his work.

1. _____ is talking and _____ to God with our minds and _____.

2. _____ is giving God thanks and _____.

3. Worshiping a creature or thing instead of _____ is _____.

God
hearts
listening
prayer
idolatry
praise
worship

Fast Facts

On the Feast of the Annunciation, we celebrate the angel appearing to Mary. The word *Annunciation* comes from *announce.* The angel Gabriel announced to Mary that she had "found favor with God" (Luke 1:30) and would be the Mother of God's Son. This feast is usually on March 25. If that day falls during Holy Week, the feast is celebrated after Easter.

What's the Word?

"Hear, O Israel! The LORD is our God, the LORD alone! Therefore, you shall love the LORD, your God, with all your heart, and with all your soul, and with all your strength. Take to heart these words which I enjoin on you today. Drill them into your children. Speak of them at home and abroad, whether you are busy or at rest." (Deuteronomy 6:4–7)

• Circle the phrase that answers: Who shall we love?

• Underline the phrase that tell how you should love God.

More to Explore

Keeping the First Commandment means that we put God first in our lives. Some Catholic men and women put God first in their lives by living in communities of prayer. They live the *monastic life.* Each monastic community lives in a place called a monastery. These men and women give their lives to God in prayer for the world. They work to support themselves in various ways, such as farming or making bread to sell. All that they do is offered to God in prayer.

DISCIPLE CHALLENGE
• How do people who live in monasteries put God first in their lives?

• Anything we do can be offered to God in prayer. What can you offer to God in prayer?

Pray Today

My God, I believe in you, I trust you, I love you.

Make it Happen

The Church teaches that we live out the First Commandment when we honor God in prayer and worship. What prayers of praise and thanksgiving can you say to express your love for God?

Take Home

The Angelus is a prayer that is prayed three times a day: 6 A.M., 12 NOON, and 6 P.M. This prayer recalls the events of the Annunciation. Pray this part of The Angelus with your family.

The angel spoke God's message to Mary, and she conceived of the Holy Spirit.

Hail Mary . . .

"I am the lowly servant of the Lord: let it be done to me according to your word."

Hail Mary . . .

88 www.webelieveweb.com

89

Fast Facts — Here are opportunities to learn even more about our faith.

What's the Word? — It's all about Scripture.

Make it Happen — We make sure that we "make faith happen" by living out what we have learned.

Take Home — We always get the chance to share our faith "at home."

There are **LOADS** of **ACTIVITIES** that make us better disciples! Just look at this additional list.

Question Corner—take a quiz

Reality Check—checking off our ideas and choices

Picture This—a great way to see and show our disciple skills

What would YOU do?—making the right choices

Celebrate!—all about worshipping God

Saint Stories—finding great role models

Now, Pass It On—invites us to witness to our faith

Don't forget to look for the Disciple Challenges—count how many you can do this year!

PROJECT DISCIPLE

You are on a journey this year to become a disciple of Jesus Christ. This year you will:

- **learn** how God's law leads us to happiness

- **pray** with heart and mind open to what Jesus asks

- **celebrate** the liturgical year in Sunday Mass and in the sacraments

- **choose** to follow a well-formed conscience

- **share** love for God and others by living the commandments

- **live out** the virtues of faith, hope and charity each day

Have a great year!

We Believe

GRADE 4 DISCIPLE CONTRACT

As a disciple of Jesus, this year I promise to

_____

_____

Name

_____

Date

_____

And remember, you can always visit **www.webelieveweb.com** for all kinds of activities, games, study guides, and resources.

Pray Learn Celebrate Share Choose Live

Growing in Jesus Christ

Seasonal Chapters

PROJECT DISCIPLE
DEAR FAMILY

In Unit 1 your child will grow as a disciple of Jesus by:

- learning that Jesus is the way, the truth and the life who teaches us how to live
- following Jesus by living the Beatitudes, and by helping the Kingdom of God to spread
- choosing to love God and others and to avoid sin
- forming a good conscience, and learning to do an examination of conscience to help make good choices
- celebrating the Sacrament of Penance and Reconciliation to receive God's forgiveness.

As a family, reflect quietly on the questions on page 47. Plan to celebrate the Sacrament of Penance and Reconciliation at the next scheduled opportunity. After you have received the sacrament, celebrate God's forgiveness together with a special meal or treat.

What Would you do?

Chapter 3 talks about making good choices. Imagine your family has an important decision to make. As a family, choose the steps your family would take to make sure you made a good decision.

Step One: _____

Step Two: _____

Step Three: _____

Other Steps: _____

Discuss ways your family could measure whether the decision made was a good one.

Reality Check

"Parents have the first responsibility for the education of their children."

(Catechism of the Catholic Church, 2223)

Question Corner Chapter 1 presents many titles for Jesus which come to us from Sacred Scripture. Look through pages 19–22, and read aloud the titles for Jesus. What title means the most to each family member? Why is it important to them?

What's the Word?

Chapter 2 presents the Beatitudes. Look at the chart on page 29. Whom do you know who lives each of the Beatitudes? Have each family member choose one of the Beatitudes to focus on and to live out this week as a disciple of Jesus.

Take Home

Be ready for this unit's Take Home:

Chapter 1: Praying to the Holy Spirit

Chapter 2: Sharing in Jesus' mission

Chapter 3: Overcoming differences

Chapter 4: Making good choices

Chapter 5: Planning a prayer corner

Jesus—the Way, the Truth, and the Life

WE GATHER

✝ **Leader:** Jesus tells us who he is. Let us listen to his words.

Reader: "I am the bread of life." (John 6:35)

All: Jesus, we believe you are the Bread of Life.

Reader: "I am the light of the world." (John 8:12)

All: Jesus, we believe you are the Light of the World.

Reader: "I am the good shepherd." (John 10:11)

All: Jesus, we believe you are the Good Shepherd.

Reader: "I am the resurrection and the life." (John 11:25)

All: Jesus, we believe you are the Resurrection and the Life.

Reader: "I am the way and the truth and the life." (John 14:6)

All: Jesus, we believe you are the Way, the Truth, and the Life.

Leader: Jesus, thank you for telling us who you are. You came into the world to show us the way to the Father.

All: Amen.

☀ Think of someone you know well. How did you get to know that person?

God sent his only Son to us.

Who is Jesus? One way we can find out about Jesus is by reading the Bible.

In the New Testament we learn that God the Father sent his only Son into the world to become one of us. The **Incarnation** is the truth that the Son of God became man. Jesus is the Son of God. He is both divine and human.

We can read about Jesus' life in the four books of the New Testament called the *Gospels*. We learn that Jesus grew up in Nazareth with his mother Mary and his foster father Joseph. Jesus loved his family. He learned about his Jewish faith and prayed to God.

As Jesus grew older, he talked to people in many towns. He taught them about God in a way that no one had before. Jesus called God "Abba." The word *abba* means "father."

Jesus once said, "I am the way and the truth and the life. No one comes to the Father except through me. If you know me, then you will also know my Father" (John 14:6–7).

Through his life and teaching, Jesus leads us to God the Father. Jesus tells us about God and the life that God wants us to share.

Imagine that you are walking with Jesus. What are you saying to him?

_____

_____

_____

Jesus shows us how to live.

Jesus wanted all people to know about God's love. Jesus treated everyone fairly. He helped those who were poor or sick. He cared for those who were lonely.

Many people were impressed by Jesus' words and actions. They wanted to know more about him. Jesus asked them to come and learn from him. Those who said yes to Jesus' call and followed him were his **disciples**.

Jesus spent about three years with his disciples. Jesus asked them to live as he did. Jesus asked them to spread his message of God's love. He knew that his disciples would need help to do this.

So when Jesus' life on earth was coming to an end, he promised that the Father would send the Holy Spirit. The Holy Spirit would help the disciples to remember and to believe all that Jesus had told them.

The Holy Spirit is the Third Person of the Blessed Trinity. The **Blessed Trinity** is the Three Persons in One God: God the Father, God the Son, and God the Holy Spirit.

 Imagine that you are walking with Jesus. What are some things he is telling you?

_____

_____

_____

_____

_____

Key Words

Incarnation (p. 260)

disciples (p. 259)

Blessed Trinity (p. 259)

21

Jesus Christ is our Savior.

God created people to share in his love and to live in his friendship. However, the first human beings turned away from God's love and disobeyed him. They committed the first sin. This first sin is called **Original Sin**. Everyone is born with Original Sin. Original Sin makes it harder for us to love and obey God.

Even though they had sinned, God did not turn away from his people. God promised to save them from sin. He sent his only Son to save all people. Jesus is the Son of God who came to take away the sin of the world.

By his dying on the cross and rising to new life, Jesus saves all people from sin. **Savior** is a title given to Jesus because he died and rose to save us from sin. Because of Jesus we can live in God's love forever.

Key Words

Original Sin (p. 260)

Savior (p. 261)

Church (p. 259)

grace (p. 260)

Reflect on what you know about Jesus. What is one thing about Jesus that is very important to you?

As a group decide one way to show others that Jesus is important to you.

The disciples spread the Good News of Jesus Christ.

After Jesus ascended to his Father in Heaven, the Holy Spirit was sent to strengthen the disciples.

The day on which the Holy Spirit came to the disciples is called *Pentecost*. The Holy Spirit helped the disciples to believe that Jesus was truly the Christ.

The disciples went everywhere teaching about Jesus. They wanted others to believe in him as the Christ and to be baptized. Many people who heard their message were baptized. This was the beginning of the Church.

The **Church** is the community of people who are baptized in Jesus Christ and follow his teachings. Baptism makes us members of the Church. Baptism frees us from Original Sin and from any sins we may have committed. In Baptism we are given new life. This new life is a share in God's own life.

The gift of God's life in us is **grace**. Grace helps us to be Jesus' disciples. As disciples we remember how Jesus lived. We work together to live as he did. When we follow the example of Jesus and share his love, we help the Church to grow.

WE RESPOND

Complete these statements.

I am the community of people who are baptized and follow Jesus Christ.

I am the

— — — — — —.

I am the day that the Holy Spirit came upon the disciples.

I am

— — — — — — — — — — —.

I am the gift of God's life.

I am

— — — — —.

The first disciples shared all they knew about Jesus. What can you share about Jesus today?

_____

_____

_____

23

PROJECT

Show What *you* Know

Write the letter that matches each 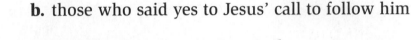 with its definition.
One word does not have a match. Add the missing definition.

1. Blessed Trinity _____
2. Church _____
3. disciples _____
4. grace _____
5. Savior _____
6. Original Sin _____
7. Incarnation _____

a. the truth that the Son of God became man

b. those who said yes to Jesus' call to follow him

c. the Three Persons in One God

d. the first sin committed by the first human beings

e. the gift of God's life in us

f. the community of people who are baptized and follow Jesus Christ

g. _____

Fast Facts

The first Sunday after Pentecost is Trinity Sunday. This day celebrates the Blessed Trinity— Three Persons in One God: God the Father, God the Son, and God the Holy Spirit.

What's *the* Word?

"After this [Jesus] went out and saw a tax collector named Levi sitting at the customs post. He said to him, 'Follow me.' And leaving everything behind, he got up and followed him." (Luke 5:27–28)

↳ **DISCIPLE CHALLENGE**

- What did Levi do when Jesus said to him, "Follow me"?

  _____

- What would people have to "leave behind" to follow Jesus today?

  _____

DISCIPLE

Pray
Learn
Celebrate
Share
Choose
Live

More to Explore

Dorothy Day wanted to help people who were homeless or hungry. She stood up for peace and against injustice. She started a soup kitchen to feed the poor in New York City. Following her example, people did the same in other cities. Dorothy Day helped to begin the Catholic Worker Movement. This group feeds hungry people, works for justice, and continues the work of Jesus in the world. Dorothy Day said yes to Jesus' call and followed him. In 2000, the Church began the process of declaring Dorothy Day a saint.

DISCIPLE CHALLENGE

• Underline the sentences that tell how Dorothy Day was a disciple of Jesus.

• Circle the name of the group that Dorothy Day helped to begin.

Pray Today

Holy Spirit, make me a stronger disciple of Jesus. Help me to

_____

_____

_____

_____

Amen.

Take Home

Pray this prayer of Saint Augustine with your family this week.

"Breathe in me, O Holy Spirit, that my thoughts may all be holy.
Act in me, O Holy Spirit, that my work, too, may be holy.
Draw my heart, O Holy Spirit, that I love but what is holy.
Strengthen me, O Holy Spirit, to defend all that is holy.
Guard me, then, O Holy Spirit, that I always may be holy.
Amen."

CHAPTER TEST

Circle the correct answer.

1. The truth that the Son of God became man is the _____.

   Blessed Trinity   Incarnation   Pentecost

3. The _____ is the Three Persons in One God.

   Blessed Trinity   Holy Spirit   Incarnation

2. Because Jesus died and rose to save us from sin, he is our _____.

   disciple   Blessed Trinity   Savior

4. The gift of God's life in us is _____.

   grace   Savior   sin

Complete the following.

5. The community of people who are baptized and follow Jesus Christ is the

   _____.

6. The people who said yes to Jesus' call and followed him were his

   _____.

7. The first human beings committed the first sin which is called

   _____.

8. Stories about Jesus' life are in the books of the New Testament called the

   _____.

Write a sentence to answer each question.

9. What happened on Pentecost?

   _____

10. What happens to us when we are baptized?

   _____

Jesus Leads Us to Happiness

WE GATHER

✝ **Leader:** Let us listen to what Jesus promises to those who trust in his ways.

Reader: "When he saw the crowds, he went up the mountain, and after he had sat down, his disciples came to him. He began to teach them, saying:

'Blessed are the poor in spirit,
    for theirs is the kingdom of
    heaven.
Blessed are they who mourn,
    for they will be comforted.'"

(Matthew 5:1–4)

🎵 **Blest Are They**

Refrain:
Rejoice and be glad!
Blessed are you, holy are you!
Rejoice and be glad!
Yours is the kingdom of God!

"Blest Are They," David Haas. Text: The Beatitudes.
©1985, G.I.A. Publications, Inc. All rights reserved.
Used with permission.

Reader:

"Blessed are the meek,
    for they will inherit the land.
Blessed are they who hunger
    and thirst for righteousness,
    for they will be satisfied."

(Matthew 5:5–6)

(Refrain)

Reader:

"Blessed are the merciful,
    for they will be shown mercy.
Blessed are the clean of heart,
    for they will see God."

(Matthew 5:7–8)

(Refrain)

Reader:

"Blessed are the peacemakers,
    for they will be called
    children of God.
Blessed are they who are
    persecuted for the sake of
    righteousness,
    for theirs is the kingdom
    of heaven."

(Matthew 5:9–10)

(Refrain)

☀ Think of someone you trust. Why do you trust that person?

Jesus trusted God his Father.

As Jesus was beginning his work, he went to the desert to pray. While Jesus was there, the Devil tempted him. The Devil wanted Jesus to stop trusting God his Father. But Jesus' trust in his Father was very strong. Jesus told the Devil to go away. He said, "It is written:

'The Lord, your God, shall you worship and him alone shall you serve'"
(Matthew 4:10).

Jesus showed his trust in God his Father through prayer. Sometimes Jesus went off by himself to pray. Other times he prayed among his disciples. Jesus prayed when he healed and forgave people, too. He prayed: "Father, I thank you for hearing me. I know that you always hear me" (John 11:41–42).

On the night before he died, Jesus prayed, "Father, if you are willing, take this cup away from me; still, not my will but yours be done" (Luke 22:42). By this prayer Jesus showed that even in his suffering he trusted in God his Father. Because of this trust, Jesus was able to do his Father's will.

No matter what is happening in our lives, Jesus wants us to trust in God's love as he did. He asks us to live as the Father wants us to live. He asks us to be at peace. **Peace** is the freedom that comes from loving and trusting God and respecting all people.

How can we show that we trust in God?

Jesus taught the Beatitudes.

The **Beatitudes** are teachings of Jesus that describe the way to live as his disciples. We learn from the Beatitudes that God offers hope to every person. We each have a reason to trust in God's love.

In the Beatitudes the word *blessed* means "happy." Jesus explains in the Beatitudes that we will be happy when we love God and trust him as Jesus did.

Jesus has a message for those who live the Beatitudes. He says, "Rejoice and be glad, for your reward will be great in heaven" (Matthew 5:12).

In the third column write what you can do to live each Beatitude. Share your examples.

The Beatitudes	Living the Beatitudes	I can . . .
"Blessed are the poor in spirit, for theirs is the kingdom of heaven.	We are "poor in spirit" when we depend on God and make God more important than anyone or anything else in our lives.	
Blessed are they who mourn, for they will be comforted.	We "mourn" when we are sad because of the selfish ways people treat one another.	
Blessed are the meek, for they will inherit the land.	We are "meek" when we are patient, kind, and respectful to all people, even those who do not respect us.	
Blessed are they who hunger and thirst for righteousness, for they will be satisfied.	We "hunger and thirst for righteousness" when we search for justice and treat everyone fairly.	
Blessed are the merciful, for they will be shown mercy.	We are "merciful" when we forgive others and do not take revenge on those who hurt us.	
Blessed are the clean of heart, for they will see God.	We are "clean of heart" when we are faithful to God's teachings and try to see God in all people and in all situations.	
Blessed are the peacemakers, for they will be called children of God.	We are "peacemakers" when we treat others with love and respect and when we help others to stop fighting and make peace.	
Blessed are they who are persecuted for the sake of righteousness, for theirs is the kingdom of heaven."	We are "persecuted for the sake of righteousness" when others disrespect us for living as disciples of Jesus and following his example.	

Key Words

peace (p. 260)

Beatitudes (p. 259)

Jesus taught about the Kingdom of God.

We learn from the Gospels that the Kingdom of God was an important part of Jesus' teaching. The **Kingdom of God** is the power of God's love active in the world. This power is shown in Jesus' words and actions.

Jesus taught that the Kingdom of God would grow if people believed in and shared God's love. Once he tried to explain to his disciples that the Kingdom of God had already begun.

Key Words

Kingdom of God (p. 260)

justice (p. 260)

mission (p. 260)

📖 Luke 17:20–21

Jesus was once asked when the Kingdom of God would come. He answered, "The coming of the kingdom of God cannot be observed, and no one will announce, 'Look, here it is,' or, 'There it is.' For behold, the kingdom of God is among you" (Luke 17:20–21).

Jesus wanted his disciples to know that God's love was a powerful force among them. Jesus showed them that God's Kingdom is a kingdom of love and justice. **Justice** means respecting the rights of others and giving them what is rightfully theirs.

When we are forgiving, merciful, just, and faithful to God, we help to build the Kingdom of God. As more and more people receive God's love and live as Jesus did, the Kingdom of God grows. It will continue to grow until Jesus returns in glory at the end of time.

👤 What are some signs that God's Kingdom is growing today?

Jesus' disciples share his mission.

Jesus spread the message of God's love everywhere he went. This was Jesus' work, or mission. He asked his disciples to do the same work.

After Jesus' Ascension, the disciples continued Jesus' work. Their **mission** was to share the Good News of Jesus Christ and to spread the Kingdom of God. This is how they carried out their mission:

- They told others the Good News that Jesus is the Son of God who died and rose to save us from sin.

- They baptized those who heard the Good News and believed.

- They gathered together to praise God and break bread as Jesus did at the Last Supper.

- They showed by their words and actions that God's love was active in their lives and in the world.

- They reached out to the poor and healed the sick and suffering.

The mission of the first disciples is the mission of the Church today. We, too, are called to continue Jesus' work. Like the first disciples we do not do this alone. Through Baptism, we are joined to all the members of the Church. At the Eucharist we receive Christ's Body and Blood. We are strengthened and led by the Holy Spirit to carry out Christ's mission.

WE RESPOND

In groups talk about some of the ways people your age can live our mission as disciples of Jesus. Then illustrate here one thing you and your family will do this week.

As Catholics...

Your Catholic faith is not a private matter between you and God. You have a role to play in the mission of the Church. The Church stands up for those who are unjustly treated or denied their basic needs. The Beatitudes teach all people to do this. Right now you can pray for people who need help. You can also join with other members of the Church to work for peace and justice for all people.

Find out how the members of your parish work for peace and justice.

![Pray Learn Celebrate Share Choose Live]

PROJECT

Show What you Know

In the Word Bank, write the  for each definition below. Then find and circle the word in the letter box.

1. The freedom that comes from loving and trusting God and respecting all people

2. The teachings of Jesus that describe the way to live as his disciples

3. The power of God's love active in the world

4. Respecting the rights of others and giving them what is rightfully theirs

5. The work of sharing the Good News of Jesus Christ and spreading the Kingdom of God

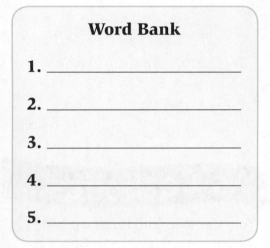

Word Bank

1. _____

2. _____

3. _____

4. _____

5. _____

```
D Q C Y Z N T P E A C E
D O G F O M O D G N I K
P U N G G R S I O A R A
V R P X M I B J S T N R
H V C V L W V J C S P X
Q U X E C I T S U J I Y
B E A T I T U D E S B M
```

Make it Happen

Decide on specific actions that will help you to continue the work of Jesus this week. List them here.

_____

_____

_____

Fast Facts

The Beatitudes are the beginning of Jesus' Sermon on the Mount. Jesus spoke this sermon on a mountain near Capernaum, which is a town on the shore of the Sea of Galilee.

DISCIPLE

Pray
Learn
Celebrate
Share
Choose
Live

More to Explore

El Salvador is a country in Central America. Oscar Romero was an archbishop in El Salvador during the 1970s. As archbishop, he saw how the poor people were suffering and dying from hunger and war. Archbishop Romero served and spoke out to defend the Church and the poor. There were some people who wanted to stop him from teaching about peace and justice. One day while celebrating Mass, he was killed. But his life had been a living example of the Beatitudes.

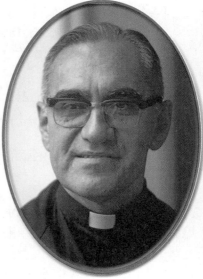

DISCIPLE CHALLENGE

• Which Beatitude do you think best describes the life of Archbishop Romero?

_____

• Why?

_____

_____

What's the Word?

Jesus gathered the Apostles and "sent them to proclaim the kingdom of God and to heal [the sick]. He said to them, 'Take nothing for the journey, neither walking stick, nor sack, nor food, nor money, and let no one take a second tunic' " (Luke 9:2–3).

DISCIPLE CHALLENGE

• Who did Jesus send out on a mission?

_____

• What did Jesus send them to do?

_____

Take Home

With your family:
• review how the disciples' mission was to continue the work of Jesus (see page 31).
• choose one way your family can share in Jesus' mission this week. Write it here.

_____

_____

_____

CHAPTER TEST

Complete each sentence.

1. The _____ are teachings of Jesus that describe the way to live as Jesus' disciples.

2. The freedom that comes from loving and trusting God and respecting all people is _____.

3. The _____ of the disciples was to share the Good News and to spread the Kingdom of God.

4. In the Beatitudes, the word *blessed* means "_____."

Write True or False for the following sentences. Then change the false sentences to make them true.

5. _____ Jesus stopped trusting God when he was tempted by the Devil.

_____

6. _____ We learn from the Beatitudes that God offers hope to every person.

_____

7. _____ The Kingdom of God is the power of God's love active in the world.

_____

8. _____ The Church today does not continue the mission of the first disciples.

_____

Write a sentence to answer each question.

9. What is one way Jesus' disciples continued his work after his Ascension?

_____

10. What did Jesus teach about the way the Kingdom of God would grow?

_____

Sin in Our World

WE GATHER

✞ **Leader:** Imagine yourself alone walking down a long path. You are shaded by large trees. You hear birds chirping. You see beautiful flowers growing along the path.

As you look down the path, you see someone. It is Jesus! He is looking right at you. His eyes are loving and inviting. He asks you these questions:

Reader: "Do you want to be my disciple? Will you choose to follow me?"

Leader: Take time to think about the way you would answer Jesus.

(silent meditation)

🎵 **Come, Follow Me**

Refrain:
Come, follow me, come, follow me.
I am the way, the truth, and the life.
Come, follow me, come, follow me.
I am the light of the world, follow me.

You call us to serve with a generous
　heart;
in building your kingdom each one
　has a part.
Each person is special in your kingdom
　of love.
Yes, we will follow you, Jesus! (Refrain)

☀ What are some of the choices you make at home and at school?

God gives us the freedom to choose.

When God created us he gave us the gift of free will. **Free will** is the freedom to decide when and how to act. We use our free will when we think for ourselves and make decisions.

God wants us to follow his law to love him, ourselves, and others. However, God does not force us to do this.

The choices people make that help them to know, love, and serve God are good choices. Yet sometimes people choose things that lead them away from God's love. These kinds of choices are sins. **Sin** is a thought, word, or action against God's law.

Sometimes it may seem easier or more fun to do things that are not good. So people may be tempted to do these things. A **temptation** is an attraction to choose sin. Temptation is not a sin, but choosing to give in to temptation is a sin.

Imagine that you have been asked to make a public service announcement on a radio program. Together make up a jingle that encourages people to be strong and not to give in to temptation.

Sin leads us away from God.

Because we have free will, we are responsible for our choices. If we choose to do something that leads us away from God, we commit a personal sin. When we sin, we fall short of being the person God wants us to be. However, there are many people in our lives who can help us to make good choices. Most importantly, we can always call on God to help us to choose what is good.

Every sin weakens our friendship with God and others. Some people commit very serious sins. A very serious sin that breaks a person's friendship with God is a **mortal sin**. To commit mortal sin someone must freely choose to do something that he or she knows is seriously wrong. Those who commit mortal sin lose grace. Yet God never stops loving them.

A less serious sin that hurts a person's friendship with God is **venial sin**. Venial sins hold people back from being as good as God made them to be. However, those who commit venial sin still have God's gift of grace.

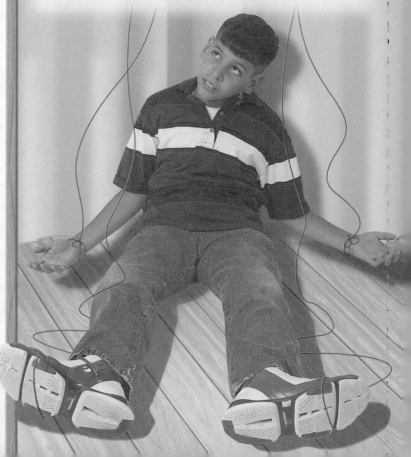

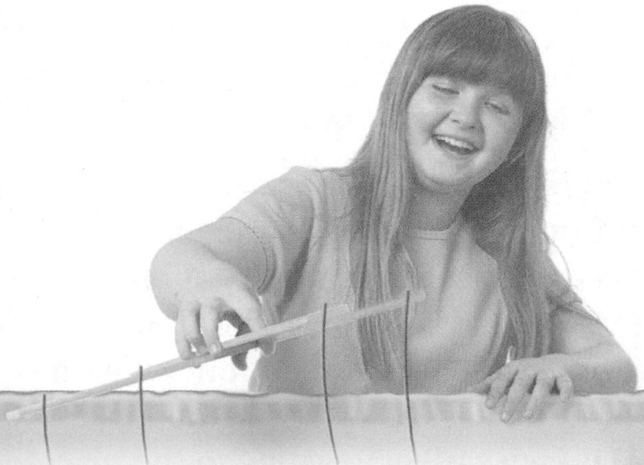

If our choices lead us away from God, we need to ask for his forgiveness. God's love and forgiveness are always there to heal and strengthen us, especially through the sacraments.

As Catholics...

In 1854, Blessed Pope Pius IX declared the Immaculate Conception of Mary, the Mother of Jesus, an official teaching of the Catholic Church. This teaching means that from the very first moment of her life, Mary was free from Original Sin. She was full of God's grace. We celebrate Mary's Immaculate Conception on December 8.

How does your parish celebrate this feast of Mary?

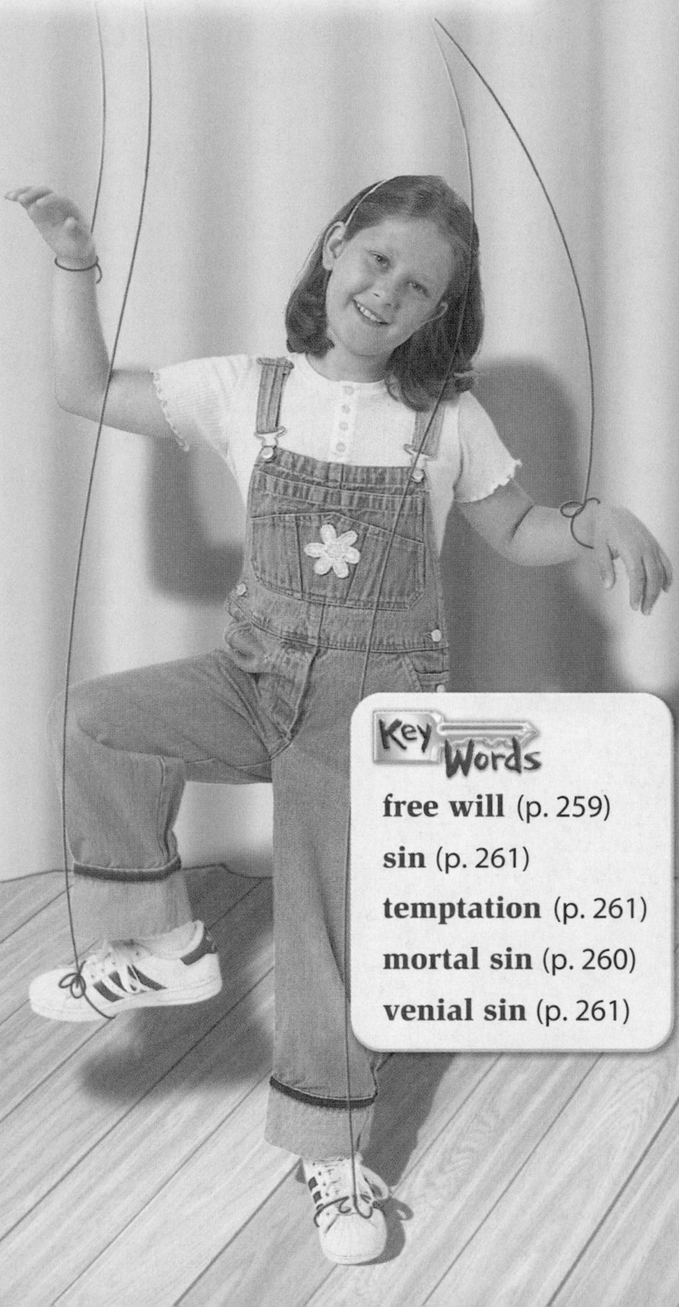

Key Words

free will (p. 259)
sin (p. 261)
temptation (p. 261)
mortal sin (p. 260)
venial sin (p. 261)

What can help us to make good choices?

Sins can be things people do or fail to do.

Every day, people try to love God and others. But sometimes people act in ways that offend God and other people. These kinds of offenses are called *sins of commission*. People actually *do* something wrong.

People can also sin by what they do *not do*. These kinds of sins are called *sins of omission*. For example, people may sin by *not* honoring God or *not* respecting others.

When we celebrate the Sacrament of Penance and Reconciliation, we ask God to forgive us for the wrongs that we do and for what we fail to do. We also ask for forgiveness at Mass when we pray: "I have greatly sinned, in my thoughts and in my words, in what I have done and in what I have failed to do."

In the Gospel of Luke we find the following story that Jesus told.

"A man fell victim to robbers as he went down from Jerusalem to Jericho. They stripped and beat him and went off leaving him half-dead. A priest happened to be going down that road, but when he saw him, he passed by on the opposite side. Likewise a Levite came to the place, and when he saw him, he passed by on the opposite side. But a Samaritan traveler who came upon him was moved with compassion at the sight. He approached the victim, poured oil and wine over his wounds and bandaged them. Then he lifted him up on his own animal, took him to an inn and cared for him." (Luke 10:30–34)

The Samaritan made the choice to help the man who had been robbed. The priest and the Levite chose not to. Jesus asks us to choose to love God and one another. He teaches us how to overcome sin by turning to God the Father and following his will. He gives us the Holy Spirit to strengthen us. Jesus promises us that we can always count on God's mercy.

Describe the actions of the Samaritan. How can we act more like the Samaritan?

We are called to value and respect all people.

Human beings do not live their lives alone. We live with others in a society, or community.

Jesus' life is our example of how to live in society. He valued and respected all human beings. He went out of his way to care for those who were poor, young, old, sick, sinners, and from other countries. Jesus taught us that we are all children of God. These words from Saint Paul remind us of Jesus' teachings:

"For through faith you are all children of God in Christ Jesus. For all of you who were baptized into Christ have clothed yourselves with Christ. . . . You are all one in Christ Jesus." (Galatians 3:26–28)

As children of God it is important to remember that every person is created in God's image. Sometimes people forget this. Sometimes they lose sight of the equality of all people. They disregard the human dignity of others. They cooperate, or take part in, *social sin*. This happens for many reasons. Here are a few:

- People are afraid to speak out against injustices.

- People only care about problems (for example, poverty) if they are affected by them.

- Their life is better if the social sin exists. For example, people might make more money themselves by not paying their own workers a fair wage.

Social sin happened in Jesus' time, too. Jesus knew that there was hatred between Jews and Samaritans. When he told the story about the Samaritan, he was asking the people to put aside their differences and help one another.

As disciples of Jesus we should not accept social sin. Our lives should show that we value and respect all human beings.

WE RESPOND

Read this statement:

Sometimes people are ignored or treated unjustly because of their skin color, nationality, gender, age, or religion.

In groups, discuss a specific example of the statement. List some ways we can correct this injustice. Then role-play one of these ways.

_____

_____

_____

_____

_____

_____

_____

_____

_____

Pray
Learn
Celebrate
Share
Choose
Live

PROJECT

Show What *you* Know

Write a paragraph using the  Key Words learned in this chapter.

_____

_____

_____

free will

sin

temptation

mortal sin

venial sin

What Would *you* do?

Arnie is the school bully. All semester long he has been picking on Joey who is half his size. Today at lunch, Arnie is making fun of Joey. A lot of your friends are laughing or ignoring the situation. You decide to

_____

_____

Question Corner

What prayers do you pray when trying to make good choices?

❏ Our Father

❏ Act of Contrition

❏ Hail Mary

❏ _____

❏ _____

Pray Today

Jesus, help me to listen when people I trust talk to me about my choices. Amen.

DISCIPLE

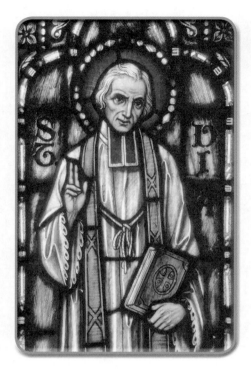

Saint Stories

John Vianney was ordained a priest in 1815 in France. He soon became famous for his ministry to sinners. He often heard confessions for sixteen hours a day. He wanted to help people to seek God's forgiveness. He was canonized a saint in 1925. Today, he is the patron saint of parish priests. Saint John Vianney's feast day is August 4.

↳ DISCIPLE CHALLENGE

- Underline the sentence that describes why Saint John Vianney wanted to minister to sinners.

- Circle the group for whom Saint John Vianney is a patron saint.

What's the Word?

Review the story of the Samaritan (page 38).

After telling the story of the Samaritan, Jesus asked the scholar, "Which of these three, in your opinion, was neighbor to the robbers' victim? He answered, 'The one who treated him with mercy.' Jesus said to him, 'Go and do likewise' " (Luke 10:36–37).

↳ DISCIPLE CHALLENGE

- Underline the phrase that tells how we should treat our neighbor.

- How did the Samaritan show that he valued and respected people?

_____

_____

Take Home

In the story of the Samaritan, Jesus teaches us that people can put aside differences and help one another. With your family, discuss a specific example where differences need to be overcome. What can your family do?

_____

_____

_____

_____

CHAPTER TEST

Circle the correct answer.

1. An attraction to choose sin is a _____.

   commission   omission   temptation

2. Sin that hurts our friendship with God is _____.

   venial sin   free will   temptation

3. Serious sin that breaks our friendship with God is _____.

   venial sin   temptation   mortal sin

4. When we fail to do something good we may commit a sin of _____.

   omission   commission   temptation

Write the letter of the phrase that defines each of the following.

5. _____ free will

6. _____ sin of commission

7. _____ social sin

8. _____ mortal sin

a. happens when we lose sight of the equality of all people and disregard their human dignity

b. breaks friendship with God, is seriously wrong, and causes the loss of grace

c. the freedom to decide when and how to act

d. when people actually do something wrong that offends God and others

Write a sentence to answer each question.

9. What is one thing Jesus taught us in the story of the Samaritan?

   _____

10. What should we remember about God's love and forgiveness?

   _____

Our Conscience, Our Guide

WE GATHER

✝ **Leader:** Sometimes we forget that no matter where we are, God is with us. He knows us better than anyone else does.

"LORD, you have probed
        me, you know me:
you know when I sit
        and stand;
you understand my
        thoughts from afar.
My travels and my rest
        you mark;
with all my ways you
        are familiar" (Psalm 139:1–3).

All: God our Father, thank you for knowing us so well.

Leader: When we are at home or at school,

All: you are with us, God.

Leader: When we are happy or have a problem,

All: you are with us, God.

Leader: When we have to make a decision,

All: you are with us, God.

Leader: We praise you, God, for knowing us so well and for being with us always.

All: Amen.

☀ How do you stay close to your family and friends?

God calls us to be close to him.

Through our Baptism each of us is called to become more like Jesus. We are called to follow the example of Jesus who always remained close to God his Father.

When we think, speak, and act as Jesus did, we become more like him. Yet, sometimes we do not follow Jesus' example. Instead of moving closer to God, we move farther away from him.

Once Jesus told this story about a father and a son.

"A man had two sons, and the younger son said to his father, 'Father, give me the share of your estate that should come to me.' . . . When he had freely spent everything, a severe famine struck that country, and he found himself in dire need. . . . Coming to his senses he thought, 'How many of my father's hired workers have more than enough food to eat, but here am I, dying from hunger. I shall get up and go to my father and I shall say to him, "Father, I have sinned against heaven and against you. I no longer deserve to be called your son; treat me as you would treat one of your hired workers."' So he got up and went back to his father. While he was still a long way off, his father caught sight of him, and was filled with compassion. He ran to his son, embraced him and kissed him." (Luke 15:11–12, 14, 17–20)

Jesus told this story to remind us that God is our loving Father. When we forget his love or turn away from it, God is always ready to welcome us back as his children.

List some words you would use to describe the father and the son in the story Jesus told.

_____

_____

_____

_____

How is God like the father in the story? How are we sometimes like the son in the story?

God gives us the gift of conscience.

God loves each of us and wants to share his life with us. He wants us to be close to him. If at times our choices lead us away from God, he calls us back to him. He calls us to turn away from sin and to live a life of goodness and love.

How do we know whether the things we do are good or sinful? To help us, God has given us a conscience. Our **conscience** is the ability to know the difference between good and evil, right and wrong. It is like an inner voice that helps us to choose good over evil.

Conscience works in three ways:

- It works *before* we make decisions. It helps us know what is good. It helps us consider the results of our choices.

- It works *while* we are making the decision. It brings about feelings of peace or discomfort depending on the choices we have made.

- It works *after* we make decisions. It enables us to judge, as good or evil, the decisions we have made.

How would our world be different if no one had a conscience?

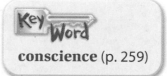

conscience (p. 259)

45

We form our conscience.

Conscience is a gift from God. In a letter Saint Paul wrote to Timothy about following the teachings of Christ, he said:

"The aim of this instruction is love from a pure heart, a good conscience, and a sincere faith" (1 Timothy 1:5).

A good conscience leads us to be truthful and fair. It guides us to make decisions that are based on the actions and teachings of Jesus. A good conscience helps us to live the way God created us to live.

Forming a good conscience is our responsibility. This responsibility continues throughout our lives.

Think about a time when you had a difficult decision to make. How did your conscience guide you?

_____

_____

A good conscience is formed by . . .

- listening to God the Holy Spirit

- asking your parents or guardians, priests, teachers, and catechists in the Church to help you

- following the good example of a life of one of the saints

- deepening your love for God

- learning more about God through Scripture

- learning more about God through Church teachings.

We examine our conscience.

No matter how busy we are, it is important to think about the things we do and say every day. An **examination of conscience** is the act of determining whether the choices we have made showed love for God, ourselves, and others.

Examining our conscience can help us to think about what we will say and do before we act. The more we examine our conscience the easier it is to hear and follow our conscience.

But how can we examine our conscience? First, we try to think about the ways we have loved God and others. We think about the ways we are living as disciples of Jesus and as members of the Church.

Next, we ask ourselves whether we have sinned, either by *doing* things that we know are wrong, or by *not doing* the good things that we could have done. We ask the Holy Spirit to help us to judge the goodness of our thoughts, words, and actions.

We can examine our conscience any time. One possible time is before we fall asleep at night. Another time is when we celebrate the Sacrament of Penance and Reconciliation.

When we examine our conscience we can thank God for giving us the strength to make good choices. Reflecting on the choices we have made helps us to make choices that bring us closer to God.

WE RESPOND

Pray to the Holy Spirit for guidance in examining your conscience. Then ask yourself the following questions:

How have I shown love, or failed to show love, for God in my thoughts, words, and actions?

How have I shown love, or failed to show love, for others in my thoughts, words, and actions?

How have I shown love, or failed to show love, for myself as a person made in God's image?

examination of conscience (p. 259)

As Catholics...

We do not form our conscience alone. The Church helps us in many ways. One way is through her teachings. The pope and the bishops have the authority to teach us in Jesus' name. They rely on Scripture and Tradition to help Catholics form their consciences.

What are some things that the pope and bishops teach us?

PROJECT

Show What *you* Know

Color only the letter spaces with ◆. Unscramble those letters to find the word to answer the two clues.

◆ i	● t	◆ c	● u	◆ c
● a	◆ n	● b	◆ o	● r
◆ e	● v	◆ c	● y	◆ n
● u	◆ s	● k	◆ e	● p

1. _____ is a gift from God that is the ability to know the difference between good and evil, right and wrong.

2. We examine our _____ when we determine whether the choices we have made showed love for God, ourselves, and others.

Pray Today

Come, Holy Spirit, be my guide as I try to follow my conscience. Amen.

Make *it* Happen

One of Jesus' teachings is "Do to others whatever you would have them do to you" (Matthew 7:12). Design a bumper sticker to remind others of this teaching.

DISCIPLE

Saint Stories

Sir Thomas More was born in England in 1477. He became a successful lawyer and scholar. King Henry VIII appointed him chancellor of England. When King Henry demanded to be the Head of the Church in England, he forced the people to accept this. But in following his conscience, Sir Thomas More could not accept this. So King Henry had him put to death.

Thomas More became a saint because he followed his conscience, the teachings of Christ, and the teachings of the Church. He is the patron saint of lawyers. His feast day is June 22. Learn more about saints. Visit *Lives of the Saints* at **www.webelieveweb.com.**

↳ DISCIPLE CHALLENGE

- Underline the phrase that tells why Thomas More could not accept King Henry VIII as Head of the Church.

- Circle the group for whom Saint Thomas More is a patron saint.

What's *the* Word?

"If we acknowledge our sins, he [God] is faithful and just and will forgive our sins and cleanse us from every wrongdoing."
(1 John 1:9)

- What will God do when we are sorry for our sins and confess them?

_____

_____

- Underline the phrase that describes God.

Take Home

You can work together as a family to form good consciences. Decide on a one-word reminder, such as "Holiness," or "Pray," or "Love." Make this word into a sign. Hang this sign in your kitchen or family room. When you and your family see the sign, it will be a reminder to make good choices at home.

CHAPTER TEST

**Write True or False for the following sentences.
Then change the false sentences to make them true.**

1. _____ The Holy Spirit can help us to form our conscience.

   _____

2. _____ The ability to know the difference between good and evil, right and wrong, is called our communion.

   _____

3. _____ Forming our conscience involves listening to trusted adults.

   _____

4. _____ We can examine our conscience only once a year.

   _____

Circle the correct answer.

5. Forming a good conscience is _____ responsibility.

   Jesus'   our   the Holy Spirit's

7. A good conscience calls us to turn away from _____.

   peace   sin   God

6. A good conscience leads us to be _____.

   truthful   sinful   dishonest

8. God is _____ ready to welcome us back to him.

   always   sometimes   never

Write a sentence to answer each question.

9. What did Jesus teach us in the story about the father and son?

   _____

10. How does our conscience help us before we make a decision?

   _____

Celebrating Penance and Reconciliation

5

WE GATHER

✝ **Leader:** Let us listen to these words from the Bible.

Reader: "Have mercy on me, God,
in your goodness . . .
Wash away all my guilt;
from my sin cleanse me."

All: A clean heart create for me, O God.

Reader: "Still, you insist on
sincerity of heart;
in my inmost being teach
me wisdom."

All: A clean heart create for me, O God.

Reader: "A clean heart create for me, God;
renew in me a steadfast spirit."
(Psalm 51:3, 4, 8, 12)

All: A clean heart create for me, O God.

Leader: God our Father, you sent your Son to show us how to be your loving children, but sometimes we fail to live as Jesus taught us. Show us your mercy and love in the Sacrament of Penance and Reconciliation.

All: Amen.

☀ How do you show that you forgive someone? How do others show that they forgive you?

Jesus tells us about God's forgiveness and love.

Jesus wanted all people to be brought back into complete friendship with God his Father. This restoring of friendship and peace is called *reconciliation*. Jesus' words and actions showed the importance of reconciliation.

In this parable Jesus taught that reconciliation is something to be celebrated:

"What man among you having a hundred sheep and losing one of them would not leave the ninety-nine in the desert and go after the lost one until he finds it? And when he does find it, he sets it on his shoulders with great joy and, upon his arrival home, he calls together his friends and neighbors and says to them, 'Rejoice with me because I have found my lost sheep.' I tell you, in just the same way there will be more joy in heaven over one sinner who repents than over ninety-nine righteous people who have no need of repentance." (Luke 15:4–7)

The word *repent* means to turn away from sin and to live the way God wants us to live. In this parable Jesus was encouraging people to repent. He taught them that if they repented God would rejoice and welcome them back.

Jesus did not ignore sinners. He offered them his Father's love and forgiveness.

Many times when Jesus forgave sinners he invited them to eat with him. This was a sign of their reconciliation with God.

Jesus reminded people how much God loved them. He encouraged them to ask for God's forgiveness and love.

In your own words describe what it means to repent and to be reconciled to God.

_____

_____

_____

We receive God's forgiveness in the Sacrament of Penance and Reconciliation.

Forgiveness was an important part of Jesus' ministry. He wanted all people to be reconciled to God. So Jesus gave his Apostles the power to forgive sins in his name:

"'Peace be with you. As the Father has sent me, so I send you.' And when he had said this, he breathed on them and said to them, 'Receive the holy Spirit. Whose sins you forgive are forgiven them, and whose sins you retain are retained.'" (John 20:21–23)

Bishops and priests continue to forgive sins in the name of Christ and through the power of the Holy Spirit. They do this in the Sacrament of Penance and Reconciliation, which we call the Sacrament of Penance.

The penitent:	The priest:

The penitent:

contrition

- has a deep sorrow for sins committed

- is truly sorry for sins and firmly intends not to sin again

- prays an Act of Contrition.

confession

- tells, or confesses, his or her sins to the priest

- talks with the priest about ways to love God and others.

penance

- is asked by the priest to say a prayer or do something that shows sorrow for his or her sins. This prayer or action is called a *penance*. It can help the penitent to make up for any harm caused by sin and to grow as a disciple of Christ.

If we sin, we can ask for God's forgiveness in this sacrament. We receive God's mercy and celebrate our friendship with him. Our friendship with God and the Church is restored.

Contrition, confession, penance, and absolution are always part of the celebration of the Sacrament of Penance. In this sacrament, the **penitent** is the person seeking God's forgiveness.

Why does God always forgive us?

Key Words

penitent (p. 260)
absolution (p. 259)

The priest:

absolution

- gives the penitent absolution. **Absolution** is God's forgiveness of sins through the words and actions of the priest.

As Catholics...

Celebrating the Sacrament of Penance strengthens our friendship with God. When we confess our sins to the priest, we tell him the thoughts, words, and actions that have led us away from God. Because we have received absolution we are able to let go of whatever might be keeping us from loving God.

It is important to remember that the priest can never, for any reason whatsoever, tell anyone what we have confessed. He is bound to secrecy by the sacrament. This secrecy is called the *seal of confession*.

Why do you think the seal of confession is important?

53

We celebrate the Sacrament of Penance.

When we are truly sorry for our sins, God forgives us. He gives us the grace to return to him and to be reconciled. We can be reconciled with God and the Church through the Sacrament of Penance.

The Church celebrates the Sacrament of Penance in different ways. One way is when a person meets individually with the priest for all the parts of the sacrament. This is called the Rite for Reconciliation of Individual Penitents.

Another way is when our parish gathers together to celebrate the sacrament. This is called the Rite for Reconciliation of Several Penitents.

Gathering for the sacrament is an important sign. It shows that God welcomes the community of faith and offers his mercy to us. We are reconciled and try to love God and one another more.

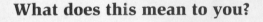

Think about this Act of Contrition. Write what this prayer, taken from the *Rite of Penance*, means to you.

Act of Contrition

My God,
I am sorry for my sins with all my heart.
In choosing to do wrong
and failing to do good,
I have sinned against you
whom I should love above all things.
I firmly intend, with your help,
to do penance,
to sin no more,
and to avoid whatever leads me to sin.
Our Savior Jesus Christ
suffered and died for us.
In his name, my God, have mercy.

What does this mean to you?

_____

_____

_____

_____

Reconciliation brings peace and unity.

When an early Christian community was having trouble, Saint Paul wrote to them. He told them to stop arguing and to start working toward reconciliation. He said, "Mend your ways, encourage one another, agree with one another, live in peace, and the God of love and peace will be with you" (2 Corinthians 13:11).

Paul wanted the early Christians to treat one another with respect. He taught them to take care of those in the community who had needs. Today we can do the same.

- In our homes we can help our parents by doing our chores.
- In our school we can pay attention in class and treat others with respect.
- In sports and games we can include everyone and try to work as a team.

- In our neighborhood we can respect the differences in the people around us.
- In our parish we can participate in the sacraments and in the parish activities that reach out to those in need.

These actions can help bring peace and unity to our communities. They can help to bring reconciliation where it is needed.

WE RESPOND

Work with a partner. Think about a time when reconciliation was needed in your school or neighborhood. Act out the ways that the people worked to restore friendship and peace. Then share your work with the class.

PROJECT

Show What *you* Know

Unscramble the letters of the  Key Words. Then use the Key Words to write two sentences about celebrating the Sacrament of Penance.

TIENPTNE _____

LNOBSAITOU _____

_____

_____

_____

Celebrate!

When Catholics are sick, at home or in the hospital, they can still receive the sacraments. A priest can visit and celebrate the Sacrament of Penance. The priest can also bring Holy Communion. These sacraments offer God's healing and strength to those who are sick.

↳ **DISCIPLE CHALLENGE** As a fourth grader, what ways can you help those who are sick? Add your own ideas.

❏ read a Bible story together

❏ bring a drink or pillow

❏ pray a decade of the Rosary

❏ make a special card or write a note

❏ _____

❏ _____

Pray
Learn
Celebrate
Share
Choose
Live

Saint Stories

Saint Alphonsus Liguori is known for his devotion to the Sacrament of Penance. He is the special saint, or patron saint, of priests who celebrate the Sacrament of Penance.

Pray this Act of Sorrow written by Saint Alphonsus Liguori.

"I love you, Jesus, my love. I love you with all my heart. I repent of having offended you. Never permit me to offend you again. Grant that I may love you always, and then do with me what you will."

Take a moment to reflect on what this prayer means to you.

Now, pass it on!

Redemptorist Fathers/Liguori Publications

Fast Facts

The Reconciliation Room is a small room designed for the individual celebration of the Sacrament of Penance. It is often located near the baptismal font. This reminds us that after Baptism, Jesus' forgiveness of our sins continues through the Sacrament of Penance.

Take Home

Make a plan to find space for a prayer corner in your home. Talk with your family members about what you will place in your prayer space.
(Make a list here.)

_____

_____

_____

_____

Invite your family to the prayer corner, and pray the prayer on page 51.

CHAPTER TEST

Write the letter of the phrase that defines each of the following.

1. _____ absolution

2. _____ penitent

3. _____ reconciliation

4. _____ repent

    a. the restoring of friendship and peace

    b. means to turn away from sin and live the way God wants us to live

    c. the person seeking God's forgiveness in the Sacrament of Penance

    d. God's forgiveness of sins through the words and actions of the priest

Circle the parts of the celebration of the Sacrament of Penance.

5. confession   beatitude   absolution   penance   contrition

Answer the following.

6. Explain briefly what the Act of Contrition is.

7. What did Jesus teach us in the parable of the shepherd and the lost sheep?

8. What is one way we can bring peace and unity to our communities?

9–10. What are the two ways the Church celebrates the Sacrament of Penance?

> "From the rising of the sun to its setting let the name of the LORD be praised."
>
> Psalm 113:3

SEASONAL

CHAPTER 6

This chapter presents an overview of the Liturgical Year.

Throughout the liturgical year we remember and celebrate Jesus Christ.

WE GATHER

✝ *God, we are your people throughout all time.*

How do we find out the day of the week, the month, and the year? Why is it important to know these things?

Are certain days special to you? Are certain times of the year special to you? Why?

WE BELIEVE

As members of the Church, we, too, have days and times of the year that are special. We remember these times in a very important way when we celebrate the liturgy, the official public prayer of the Church. The celebration of the Eucharist, also called the Mass, is liturgy. The liturgy also includes the celebration of the other sacraments and the Liturgy of the Hours. The Liturgy of the Hours is a special prayer of the Church that is prayed several times during the day.

The liturgy is so important to the life of the Church that our Church year is called the liturgical year. Throughout the liturgical year, we remember and celebrate everything about Jesus Christ: his birth, life, Death, Resurrection, and Ascension.

When we celebrate the life of Christ, we show that we believe in God the Father, the Son, and the Holy Spirit. As we go through the year with Christ, we grow in faith, hope, and love. We discover that every day of the year is a day to live in joyful hope and praise of God.

The readings we hear, the colors we see, and the songs we sing help us to know what season we are celebrating. Do you know what season we are celebrating now? Use this diagram of the liturgical year to help you to find out.

The liturgical year begins in late November or early December with the season of Advent.

Advent The season of Advent prepares us for the celebration of Jesus' first coming. Over two thousand years ago Jesus was born, the Son of God became one of us. During Advent we also celebrate that Christ is in the world today, and that Christ will come again. We watch, wait, and pray, "Come, Lord Jesus!" (Revelation 22:20).

Christmas The Christmas season begins on Christmas Day with the celebration of the birth of the Son of God. During the Christmas season we celebrate that God is with us. We rejoice because "A Son is born to us, and he is the Prince of Peace. Alleluia!"

Lent The season of Lent begins on Ash Wednesday. Lent is a special time to remember that Jesus suffered, died, and rose to new life for us. During Lent we try to become more like Jesus through prayer and acts of mercy and kindness. We pray, "Jesus, help us to follow you." In these ways we prepare for the Church's greatest celebration.

Triduum The Easter Triduum is the Church's greatest and most important celebration. The word *triduum* means "three days." During these three days, from Holy Thursday evening until Easter Sunday evening, we remember the Death of Jesus and celebrate his Resurrection. We pray, "We worship you, Lord. Through the cross you brought joy to the world."

Easter The season of Easter begins on Easter Sunday evening and continues until Pentecost Sunday. We sing for joy because "Christ is risen, and makes all things new. Alleluia!"

Ordinary Time The season of Ordinary Time is celebrated in two parts: the first part is between Christmas and Lent, and the second part between Easter and Advent. During this season we celebrate the whole life of Christ. We learn more about Jesus and the Christian life. We listen to God's Word and act on it. We pray, "Here am I, Lord; I come to do your will."

THE LITURGICAL YEAR

Take another look at the diagram of the liturgical year. Then work with a partner and complete this chart. Remember that some colors are used in more than one season.

color	sign of	season(s)
violet	expectation, waiting, penance	_____
white or gold	joy and light	_____
green	life and hope	_____
red	royalty, fire, death	_____

Honoring Mary and the Saints

In every liturgical season there are feast days that honor Mary, the Mother of Jesus, with special love. The Church is devoted to Mary because she is the Mother of the Son of God. We believe that she is our mother and the Mother of the Church, too. She is a great example for living as a disciple of Jesus. On her feast days we remember the ways that God blessed Mary. We recall important events in her life and in the life of Jesus.

During the liturgical year we also remember the saints—women, men, and children who have lived lives of holiness on earth and now share eternal life with God in Heaven.

The saints were faithful followers of Christ. They loved and cared for others as Jesus did. Some of the saints even died for their belief in Christ. We celebrate that their lives are examples of faith for us. We ask the saints to pray with us to God.

WE RESPOND

Work with a partner. Get a twelve-month calendar and show the liturgical season you are in as you go from January 1 to December 31. Talk about where the liturgical seasons fit into the regular calendar year. What might be happening in school, at home, or in the neighborhood during each liturgical season? Brainstorm some ways that those every day activities can help us to live in joyful hope and praise.

✚ We Respond in Prayer

Refrain: "From the rising of the sun to its setting
let the name of the LORD be praised."
(Psalm 113:3)

Reader 1: Let us give thanks for the season of Advent
and pray, "Come, Lord Jesus!" (Revelation 22:20).

All: (Refrain)

Reader 2: Let us give thanks for the Christmas season
and pray, "A Son is given to us, and he is the Prince
of Peace."

All: (Refrain)

Reader 3: Let us give thanks for the holy season of Lent
and pray, "Jesus, we will follow you wherever you go."

All: (Refrain)

Reader 4: Let us give thanks for the three days of the
Triduum, and pray, "Christ has died. Christ is risen.
Christ will come again."

All: (Refrain)

Reader 5: Let us give thanks for the season of Easter,
and pray, "Christ is risen and makes all things new.
Alleluia!"

All: (Refrain)

Reader 6: Let us give thanks for the season of Ordinary
Time and pray, "Here am I, Lord; I come to do your will."

All: (Refrain)

Leader: Let us pray. Lord, we thank you for your Church
and for all of the seasons of our liturgical year. Help us
to follow you all our days, now and forever.

All: Amen.

PROJECT DISCIPLE

Pray Learn Celebrate Share Choose Live

Show What *you* Know

Match each season of the liturgical year with the prayers that might be said during that season. See page 61 if you need help.

1. Advent _____ a. "Jesus, help us to follow you."

2. Christmas _____ b. "Here I am, Lord, I come to do your will."

3. Lent _____ c. "A Son is born to us. Alleluia!"

4. Triduum _____ d. "Come, Lord Jesus!"

5. Easter _____ e. "Lord, through the cross you brought joy to the world."

6. Ordinary Time _____ f. "Christ is risen and makes all things new. Alleluia!"

Celebrate!

We have many feasts to honor Mary during the Liturgical Year. In Advent we celebrate the *Immaculate Conception of Mary*. The *Solemnity of Mary, the Mother of God* is during the Christmas season. The *Assumption of Mary* comes during Ordinary Time. Feasts are also celebrated under Mary's titles of *Our Lady of Guadalupe*, the *Immaculate Heart of Mary*, and *Our Lady of the Rosary*. The months of May and October have been devoted to Mary.

↳ DISCIPLE CHALLENGE

• Underline the feast of Mary that occurs during Advent.

• What months are especially devoted to Mary?

Take Home

In your prayer corner, place a statue or picture of Mary. On Mary's feast days, add flowers to honor her. Then gather there with your family and pray to Mary.

Question Corner

What season of the liturgical year is the Church celebrating now?

_____

"Make known to me your ways, LORD;
teach me your paths."

Psalm 25:4

SEASONAL

CHAPTER 7

This chapter helps us to understand
the season of Ordinary Time.

During the season of Ordinary Time, we celebrate the life and teachings of Jesus Christ.

WE GATHER

✠ *Jesus, help us live in your love every day of the year.*

What do you think of when you hear the word *ordinary*? Can you think of some other words that mean the same thing?

WE BELIEVE

During the season of Ordinary Time we celebrate the whole life of Jesus Christ. We listen to his teachings about God the Father, and about his love and forgiveness. We learn what it means to be a disciple. We celebrate everything that Jesus did for us. We celebrate his life, Death, and Resurrection.

The season of Ordinary Time lasts thirty-three to thirty-four weeks. It is the longest season of the year, and is the only season that is celebrated in two parts. The first part is celebrated between the seasons of Christmas and Lent. The second part of Ordinary Time lasts many weeks and spans the time between the seasons of Easter and Advent.

Ordinary Time does not mean that every day in this season is just an ordinary day! It is called Ordinary Time because the weeks are "ordered," or named in number order. For example, the First Sunday in Ordinary Time is followed by the Second Sunday in Ordinary Time, and so on. During Ordinary Time one of the Gospels is also read in number order, chapter by chapter, so that we learn about the life of Jesus.

There are four Gospel writers, or *Evangelists*: Matthew, Mark, Luke, and John. Each year at the Sunday and weekday Masses during Ordinary Time we hear one of the Gospels of Matthew, Mark, or Luke in its entirety. So it takes three years to read all three of these Gospels. Then the cycle starts over again.

The Gospel of John is not usually read at Mass during Ordinary Time. However, it is read during the other seasons of the year.

Saint Matthew

Feast day September 21

Matthew was a tax collector. He gave up everything to follow Jesus. The Gospel of Matthew focuses in a special way on Jesus being both divine and human. Over the centuries, each Gospel was identified by a symbol. The symbol of Matthew's Gospel is an angelic young man. This symbol means that Jesus is both God and man.

Saint Mark

Feast day April 25

Mark's Gospel is the shortest one, and it may be the very first Gospel written. The symbol of Mark's Gospel is a royal winged lion. It is a symbol of kingship. Mark's Gospel has many references to Jesus as the king who has come to bring his kingdom to us.

Saint Luke

Feast day October 18

Luke wrote both a Gospel and the Acts of the Apostles. Luke's Gospel, like the Gospel of Matthew, includes the stories of Mary, Joseph, and the coming of the Son of God into the world. The symbol of Luke's Gospel is the winged ox. During the time of Jesus, an ox was an animal that was sacrificed in the Temple. In Luke's Gospel, we learn that Jesus is our new sacrifice. He offered himself to save us and because of his Death and Resurrection we have new life.

Saint John

Feast day December 27

The Evangelist John wrote a Gospel that is very different from the other three Gospels. The symbol of John's Gospel is an eagle. An eagle can see from very far away, and it carries its young on its wings. An eagle can soar high, up to the heavens. The Gospel of John helps us to see God's plan lived out in Jesus' life, Death, and Resurrection. Like an eagle, the risen Christ carries us to God.

WE RESPOND

The Evangelists spread the Good News of Jesus Christ. So, too, each of us is called to be an evangelist. As members of the Church, we spread the Good News and share our faith so that others might believe.

Look at Jesus' words written down by the Evangelists. What do these words mean to you? Rewrite these words as if Jesus were saying them today.

"Do to others whatever you would have them do to you."
(Matthew 7:12)

"Take courage, it is I, do not be afraid!" (Mark 6:50)

"Be merciful, just as [also] your Father is merciful."
(Luke 6:36)

"Love one another as I love you." (John 15:12)

✝ We Respond in Prayer

Leader: Let us celebrate the Feast of Saint Francis of Assisi.

Reader 1: Saint Francis was the son of a rich nobleman. Francis wanted to live just like Jesus. He left his riches behind and began a new community in the Church. Many people today are members of this religious community. They are called Franciscans.

Reader 2: Let us listen now to the Word of God as it is read on the Feast of Saint Francis.

"May I never boast except in the cross of our Lord Jesus Christ. Peace and mercy be to all who follow this rule. The grace of our Lord Jesus Christ be with your spirit." (Galatians 6:14, 16, 18)

Reader 3: Let us ask Saint Francis to pray for us as we try to follow Jesus. Our response after each is "Pray for us."

Francis, man of peace and lover of the poor, (Response)

Francis, poet and singer of God's creation, (Response)

Francis, protector of animals, (Response)

🎵 **Prayer of St. Francis/ Oración de San Francisco**

All: Make me a channel of your peace.
Where there is hatred, let me bring your love.
Where there is injury, your pardon, Lord,
And where there's doubt, true faith in you.

Hazme un instrumento de tu paz,
donde haya odio lleve yo tu amor,
donde haya injuria, tu perdón, Señor,
donde haya duda fe en ti.

Show What *you* Know

Draw lines connecting the Evangelist with his symbol.

1. Saint Matthew •   • winged lion

2. Saint Mark •   • eagle

3. Saint Luke •   • angelic young man

4. Saint John •   • winged ox

Which Evangelist's Gospel is NOT usually read during Ordinary Time?

_____

Saint Stories

The Feast of Saints Peter and Paul falls on June 29 during Ordinary Time. These two great saints have been honored throughout the history of the Church. Saint Peter was the Apostle chosen by Jesus to lead his Church. Saint Paul described himself as a servant of Jesus Christ, "called to be an apostle and set apart for the gospel of God." (Romans 1:1)

↳ **DISCIPLE CHALLENGE**

• Circle the phrase that tells what Jesus chose Peter to do.

• Underline the phrase that Paul used to describe himself.

Pray Today

Dear God, during this season of Ordinary Time, I remember and celebrate Jesus' life. Help me to follow Jesus in my daily life. Teach me, O Lord, and I will follow your way.
Amen.

Take Home

As a family, during the weeks of Ordinary Time, continue to learn about and celebrate the life of Jesus Christ. Have family discussions about specific things you can place in your prayer corner to help you remember that you are celebrating Ordinary Time.

UNIT TEST

Fill in the circle beside the correct answer.

1. Jesus called God *Abba*, a word that means "_____."

   ○ Father   ○ Savior   ○ Anointed One

2. In Baptism we are given _____, the gift of God's life in us.

   ○ Incarnation   ○ grace   ○ Pentecost

3. In the Beatitudes, Jesus explains that we will be happy when we love God and _____ him as Jesus did.

   ○ fear   ○ trust   ○ tempt

4. Respecting the rights of others and giving them what is rightfully theirs is _____.

   ○ peace   ○ mercy   ○ justice

5. Because we have _____, we are responsible for the choices we make.

   ○ Original Sin   ○ social sin   ○ free will

6. God gave us the gift of _____ to help us know the difference between good and evil, right and wrong.

   ○ conscience   ○ reconciliation   ○ forgiveness

7. During the celebration of the Sacrament of Penance, we pray an Act of _____.

   ○ Commission   ○ Absolution   ○ Contrition

8. In the Sacrament of Penance we receive God's _____.

   ○ forgiveness   ○ repentance   ○ confession

9. The truth that the Son of God became man is the _____.

   ○ Incarnation   ○ Blessed Trinity   ○ Beatitudes

continued on next page

Write True or False for the following sentences.
Then change the false sentences to make them true.

10. _____ *Savior* is a title given to Jesus Christ because he called disciples to follow him.

_____

11. _____ In the Beatitudes the word *blessed* means "clean of heart."

_____

12. _____ In Baptism we are given new life and become members of the Church.

_____

13. _____ A temptation is a thought, word, or action against God's law.

_____

14. _____ A sin that we commit by not doing something is called a sin of omission.

_____

15. _____ A good conscience works in three ways: before, while, and after we make a decision.

_____

16. _____ In the Sacrament of Penance, the priest gives the penitent contrition in the name of the Father, the Son, and the Holy Spirit.

_____

Write your answers to the questions on a separate sheet of paper.

17–18. What was the mission Jesus gave his disciples?

19–20. A good conscience helps us to live the way God created us to live. What are some of the things we can do to form a good conscience?

The Commandments Help Us to Love God

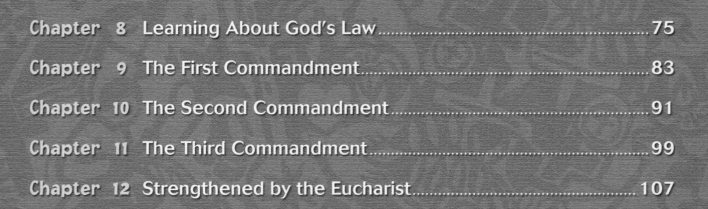

Seasonal Chapters

Chapter 13 Advent

Chapter 14 Christmas

DEAR FAMILY

In Unit 2 your child will grow as a disciple of Jesus by:

- showing love for God and others by following the Ten Commandments and the Great Commandment
- believing in the one true God, and loving him more than anything
- respecting God's name, and honoring sacred places
- keeping the Lord's Day holy by participating in Mass, relaxing, and caring for others' needs
- learning the ways to participate more fully at Mass, and to live as Jesus' disciples when we are sent forth from Mass.

What's the Word?

In Chapter 8 the children review the Ten Commandments, and also Jesus' teaching of the Great Commandment, and the new commandment which Jesus gave us at the Last Supper.

Read about Jesus giving the Great Commandment on page 78, or in your Bible (Matthew 22:34–40). Discuss why Jesus would say to the young man that this is the greatest commandment. Then read the new commandment on page 78 or in your Bible (John 13:34–35). Decide on one way you can live the new commandment this week.

Celebrate!

Prepare for the coming Sunday to be the Lord's Day in a special way. Look over the Sunday Scripture readings together, and talk about the ways you will participate in Mass. (See "This Week's Liturgy" on www.webelieveweb.com.) What Corporal or Spiritual Work of Mercy (pages 102–103) might you do on Sunday to show that your family cares for people in need?

Reality Check

"The Christian family is a communion of persons, a sign and image of the communion of the Father and the Son in the Holy Spirit."

(Catechism of the Catholic Church, 2205)

Fast Facts

One of the Corporal Works of Mercy is to visit the imprisoned. Many diocesan Catholic Charities offices or Peace and Justice Offices train volunteers to visit those who are imprisoned. These volunteers provide Bibles and opportunities to learn the faith and to pray. Say a prayer together that all those who are imprisoned will place their love and trust in God.

Question Corner

Chapters 9, 10, and 11 present the first three commandments. Talk about these commandments together. (See the chart on page 77.) How can each commandment make us happy? Which commandment is most challenging to our world today?

Take Home

Be ready for this unit's Take Home:

Chapter 8: Living out the Great Commandment

Chapter 9: Praying the Angelus

Chapter 10: Making a banner

Chapter 11: Getting ready for Mass

Chapter 12: Visiting the Most Blessed Sacrament

Learning About God's Law

WE GATHER

✝ **Leader:** Let us listen to a reading from the Book of Psalms.

Reader: "LORD, teach me the way
of your laws;
I shall observe them
with care.
Give me insight to
observe your teaching,
to keep it with all my heart.
Lead me in the path of
your commands,
for that is my delight."
(Psalm 119:33–35)

All: "LORD, teach me the way
of your laws." (Psalm 119:33)

Leader: Let us pray.
Father, we want to respect your laws. Help us to love you and our neighbors. We ask this in the name of Jesus our Lord.

All: Amen.

☀ Think of a time when someone asked you to follow some instructions. Why was it important to do as you were asked?

God calls his people.

In the Old Testament we learn about the relationship between God and his people. We read the history of God's people in the time before the birth of Jesus.

The people whom God chose as his own were called the Israelites. God showed his great love for them, and they showed their love for God. They called on God for help and guidance. They gave praise to God's name. God remembered his people and heard them. He cared for and protected them.

God's people were living in the area of the Middle East that is now the country called Israel. However, in the time of the Old Testament, this land was called Canaan. Once a great famine forced God's people to leave their homes in Canaan. They went to Egypt to find food. They stayed in Egypt, but they later lost their freedom there. God's people became slaves. They were forced to work for the pharaoh, the ruler of Egypt. God wanted his people to be free to love and worship him. So God chose Moses to lead the people out of Egypt to freedom.

📖 Exodus 3:7–10

God told Moses that he had seen the way his people were suffering in Egypt. God said, "Therefore I have come down to rescue them from the hands of the Egyptians and lead them out of that land into a good and spacious land, a land flowing with milk and honey."

Then God said to Moses, "Come, now! I will send you to Pharaoh to lead my people, the Israelites, out of Egypt" (Exodus 3:7, 8, 10).

With Moses to lead them and God guiding their way, the people left Egypt. They were heading back to Canaan, the land God had promised them.

🏃 God guided Moses and his people. Write ways God guides us today.

_____

_____

_____

The Ten Commandments are God's Laws for his people.

In the desert between Egypt and Canaan, the Israelites came to Mount Sinai. God asked Moses to climb the mountain. There God made a special agreement with Moses and the people. God promised to be their God if they would be his people. This special agreement between God and his people is called a **covenant**.

God gave us the Ten Commandments so we can know how to live a life of love. The first three commandments help us to show love and respect for God. The other seven commandments help us to show love and respect for ourselves and others.

 With a partner discuss ways to show respect for God and others.

In this covenant God promised to protect his people and to help them live in freedom. In return the Israelites promised to live as God wanted them to live. They promised to worship him, the one true God.

God gave Moses and his people the Ten Commandments. The **Ten Commandments** are the Laws of God's covenant given to Moses on Mount Sinai. The Israelites, later known as the Jewish People, followed these Laws. The Ten Commandments are God's Laws for us, too. We find them in the Old Testament.

THE TEN COMMANDMENTS

1. I AM THE LORD YOUR GOD: YOU SHALL NOT HAVE STRANGE GODS BEFORE ME.

2. YOU SHALL NOT TAKE THE NAME OF THE LORD YOUR GOD IN VAIN.

3. REMEMBER TO KEEP HOLY THE LORD'S DAY.

4. HONOR YOUR FATHER AND YOUR MOTHER.

5. YOU SHALL NOT KILL.

6. YOU SHALL NOT COMMIT ADULTERY.

7. YOU SHALL NOT STEAL.

8. YOU SHALL NOT BEAR FALSE WITNESS AGAINST YOUR NEIGHBOR.

9. YOU SHALL NOT COVET YOUR NEIGHBOR'S WIFE.

10. YOU SHALL NOT COVET YOUR NEIGHBOR'S GOODS.

Key Words

covenant (p. 259)

Ten Commandments (p. 261)

Jesus teaches us about God's Law.

God loved his people so much that he never turned away from them. When he saw his people failing, God sent prophets to remind them to keep the covenant. The prophets told the people about God's love for them. They encouraged the people to trust in God and have faith in him. They reminded the people that God had promised to save them from sin.

God kept his promise. He sent his only Son into the world to save all people from sin. Jesus is the Son of God.

When Jesus was growing up in Nazareth, he studied the teachings of the Old Testament. He learned about the covenant God made with his people. He followed the Ten Commandments. He lived his life according to the covenant.

One day someone asked Jesus, "Teacher, which commandment in the law is the greatest?" We call Jesus' answer the Great Commandment. Jesus said to the man, "You shall love the Lord, your God, with all your heart, with all your soul, and with all your mind" (Matthew 22:36, 37). This is the first part of the Great Commandment. It sums up the first three of the Ten Commandments.

Jesus also told the man, "You shall love your neighbor as yourself" (Matthew 22:39). This part of the Great Commandment sums up the Fourth through Tenth Commandments.

Jesus himself lived out the Great Commandment. He showed us that keeping the Ten Commandments means loving God above all else and loving others as ourselves.

Who are some people today who encourage us to trust in God and have faith in him?

Jesus teaches us to love one another.

On the night before he died, Jesus told his disciples, "I give you a new commandment: love one another. As I have loved you, so you also should love one another. This is how all will know that you are my disciples, if you have love for one another" (John 13:34–35).

Loving one another as Jesus did helps us to follow the Ten Commandments. Jesus was a perfect example of love for God and neighbor. He showed his love in many ways. He listened to those who were lonely. He went out of his way to help people in need. He spoke out for the freedom of all people and for those who were treated unjustly. He respected the dignity of each person.

We are called to respect the human dignity of all people. All people are created by God to share in his life and love. Each and every person has the same basic rights. We call the basic rights that all people have **human rights**.

These rights include the

- right to life. This the most basic of all human rights.

- right to faith and family

- right to education and work

- right to equal treatment and safety

- right to housing and health care.

WE RESPOND

With a partner, discuss the ways you can respect the rights of others as Jesus did. Talk about ways that we can follow Jesus' example of love for God and others. Then make a Word Find using those ways. Exchange your puzzle with another group and have them find and circle the words.

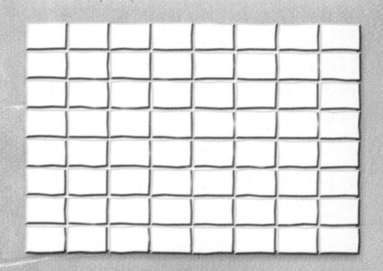

Key Word

human rights (p. 260)

As Catholics...

God sent many prophets to his people. One of the greatest of these was Isaiah. Isaiah told the people that God would never abandon them, that God would send them a Savior. Jesus is the Savior Isaiah told the people about.

Every year during Advent and Christmas, we hear the words of Isaiah: "For a child is born to us, a son is given us" (Isaiah 9:5). Jesus is the Son of God and our Savior.

PROJECT

Pray Learn Celebrate Share Choose Live

Show What *you* Know

To find the Key Words to complete each sentence, use the code below. Fill in the letter that matches each symbol.

✳	♣	★	◎	♥	⊕	✵	✱	◆	❂	⚥	◉	✤	♠	☀
A	C	D	E	G	H	I	M	N	O	R	S	T	U	V

1. The special agreement between God and his people is called a

___ ___ ___ ___ ___ ___ ___ ___ .
♣ ❂ ☀ ◎ ◆ ✳ ◆ ♣

2. The laws of God's covenant given to Moses on Mount Sinai are the

___ ___ ___ ___ ___ ___ ___ ___ ___ ___ ___ ___ ___ ___ ___ .
✤ ◎ ◆ ✤ ♣ ❂ ✱ ✱ ✳ ◆ ★ ✱ ◎ ◆ ✤ ◉

3. The basic rights that all people have are

___ ___ ___ ___ ___ ___ ___ ___ ___ ___ ___ ___ .
⊕ ♠ ✱ ✳ ◆ ⚥ ✵ ♥ ⊕ ✤ ◉

Fast Facts

The covenant that God made with Moses is still honored and lived today by the Jewish People. The Ten Commandments are part of what is called The Torah, which in Hebrew means, "The Law." The scrolls on which the law is written have a place of honor in every synagogue.

Pray Today

Holy Spirit, help me to live by the Ten Commandments. Help me to

_____

_____

_____

_____

DISCIPLE

Pray
Learn
Celebrate
Share
Choose
Live

Make *it* Happen

God calls us to respect everyone's human rights. Choose one of the human rights listed below.

- right to life
- right to faith and family
- right to education and work
- right to equal treatment and safety
- right to housing and health care

Make a plan to promote this right in your school and neighborhood this week.

_____

_____

_____

_____

What's *the* Word?

"You shall love the Lord, your God, with all your heart, with all your soul, and with all your mind." (Matthew 22:37) *"You shall love your neighbor as yourself."* (Matthew 22:39)

- Circle the phrases that answer: Who shall we love?
- Underline the phrases that tell how you should love God.

Take Home

Discuss with your family ways to live the Great Commandment. Write one way your family will love God and others this week.

_____

_____

_____

_____

81

Circle the correct answer.

1. In the Old Testament we learn about the relationship between God and _____.

   the Apostles   Jesus   the Israelites

2. A covenant is a special _____ between God and his people.

   agreement   prayer   vision

3. Jesus taught us to love God above all else and to _____ our neighbors as ourselves.

   fear   love   trust

4. The most basic of all human rights is the right to _____.

   faith   equal treatment   life

Write True or False for the following sentences.
Then change the false sentences to make them true.

5. _____ The Ten Commandments help us to live a life of love.

   _____

6. _____ The Great Commandment sums up the Ten Commandments.

   _____

7. _____ Following the first three commandments helps us to love our neighbors.

   _____

8. _____ God gave the Ten Commandments to Jesus on Mount Sinai.

   _____

Answer the following.

9. Write one way the prophets helped the Israelites.

   _____

10. Write one way Jesus showed people his love.

   _____

The First Commandment

WE GATHER

✝ **Leader:** Let us pray these words from the Book of Psalms.

Reader: "For you are great and do wondrous deeds; and you alone are God."
(Psalm 86:10)

All: Blessed be God for ever.

Reader: "Teach me, LORD, your way that I may walk in your truth, single-hearted and revering your name."
(Psalm 86:11)

All: Blessed be God for ever.

Reader: "I will praise you with all my heart, glorify your name forever, Lord my God."
(Psalm 86:12)

All: Blessed be God for ever.

Leader: God, you have shown us that you are a God of love. Since the creation of the world, you have given us all good things. May we honor you and bring glory to your holy name.

All: Amen.

☀ Think of people you are close to or look up to. How do you show them you believe in them? Why is it important that they know you believe in them?

WE BELIEVE
We believe in the one true God.

The First Commandment states that, "I am the LORD your God. You shall not have strange gods before me." In the Old Testament we read that not everyone believed in the one true God as the Israelites did. The people who believed in many gods imagined how their gods would look. They carved images of them from wood and stone.

The Israelites lived among people who worshiped these gods. So God said to his people:

"I, the LORD, am your God, who brought you out of the land of Egypt, that place of slavery. You shall not have other gods besides me. You shall not carve idols for yourselves in the shape of anything in the sky above or on the earth below or in the waters beneath the earth; you shall not bow down before them or worship them" (Exodus 20:2–5).

God asked his people to believe in him, to love him, and to honor him above all else.

Here is a special prayer the Israelites prayed. It is called the Shema. *Shĕmá* is the Hebrew word meaning "hear."

"Hear, O Israel!
The LORD is our God,
the LORD alone!
Therefore, you shall love
the LORD, your God,
with all your heart,
and with all your soul,
and with all your strength."

(Deuteronomy 6:4–5)

Today, Jews all around the world still pray the Shema every day.

Think quietly and prayerfully about these questions:

Do I try to love God above all things?

Do I really believe in, trust, and love God?

We honor the one true God.

When we live out the First Commandment, we honor God. We honor God by believing in him, praying to him, and worshiping him. We also honor God by loving others.

Prayer is listening and talking to God with our minds and hearts. Through prayer we can grow closer to God. **Worship** is giving God thanks and praise. We praise him for his goodness. We adore God and thank him for his many gifts to us. We offer our love to God.

Our greatest act of love and worship is the celebration of the Mass. At Mass we are united to Jesus, who offered himself on the cross to save us.

Key Words

prayer (p. 261)

worship (p. 261)

When we honor God we show our thanks for all that he has done for us. Compose a poem titled "Honoring God."

_____

_____

_____

_____

_____

_____

_____

_____

_____

As Catholics...

Only God is to be worshiped and adored. But we venerate, or show devotion to, Mary and the saints. The saints were holy people who honored God in their lives. We can learn about worshiping God by studying their lives. The lives of the saints show us that it is possible to love God above all things.

To what saint is your family devoted? How is this saint an example of living as a Christian?

We love God above all things.

God wants us to be happy. He wants us to have the things we need. God wants us to help others to have what they need, too.

We all need food and clothing, a place to live, and a way to travel from one place to another. We need to enjoy time with our family and friends. We need the chance to make a living.

However, the First Commandment reminds us that we need God more than anything. We must put God first in our lives. Everything we do and say should show how important God is to us.

Sometimes we put someone or something before God. If we worship a person or a thing instead of God, we are setting up a false god. Giving worship to a creature or thing instead of God is **idolatry**.

By his life and words, Jesus kept God first in his life.

Luke 4:1–8

Before Jesus began his work among the people, he went to the desert to pray. There the Devil offered Jesus all the lands of the world. He would give Jesus all their riches and power. He said to Jesus, "All this will be yours, if you worship me" (Luke 4:7). Jesus refused the Devil.

Riches and power were not important to Jesus. Nothing was more important to Jesus than serving God his Father. He loved his Father above all things. Jesus wants us to love God above all things and to serve him throughout our lives.

With a partner, list some things that people might love and honor more than God.

_____

_____

_____

We place our hope and trust in God.

Jesus wanted his followers to believe in God's love and care. Jesus taught people to trust and hope in God. When we trust and hope in God, we will be happy. Trusting and hoping in God is part of living out the First Commandment. God the Holy Spirit helps us to trust and hope. Trusting God means believing in his love for us. Putting our hope in God means we are confident in God's blessings in our lives.

The Blessed Virgin Mary, the Mother of Jesus, is a great example of hope and trust. When she was a young girl, an angel of the Lord came to her. The angel told her, "Do not be afraid, Mary, for you have found favor with God" (Luke 1:30). Mary then learned that God had chosen her to be the Mother of his Son. She must have been both amazed and confused. But Mary believed in God's love for her. So she said, "Behold, I am the handmaid of the Lord. May it be done to me according to your word" (Luke 1:38).

Mary was blessed by God. She put her hope in him and in his Son. Mary was confident of God's care for her, and was willing to do what God asked of her. In all that she did, Mary trusted God completely.

Key Word

idolatry (p. 260)

Trusting in God at all times is not always easy. There are times when we may lose sight of his love for us. Sometimes playing sports, watching television, or using the computer take so much time that God loses importance in our lives. Other times we are so happy and things are going so well that we may forget that we need God.

Call on God! God will help you to remember that you need him. Through the sacraments and the love of others, God will give you the grace to trust in him and to hope in his goodness.

WE RESPOND

Design a computer screen saver to remind yourself to follow the First Commandment.

Pray
Learn
Celebrate
Share
Choose
Live

PROJECT

Show What *you* Know

Jordan's sister hit the delete key after Jordan worked on the Key Word definitions. Use the words in the box to help Jordan restore his work.

1. _____ is talking and _____ to God

   with our minds and _____.

2. _____ is giving God thanks and _____.

3. Worshiping a creature or thing instead of _____

   is _____.

God

hearts

listening

prayer

idolatry

praise

worship

Fast Facts

On the Feast of the Annunciation, we celebrate the angel appearing to Mary. The word *Annunciation* comes from "announce." The angel Gabriel announced to Mary that she had "found favor with God" (Luke 1:30) and would be the Mother of God's Son. This feast is usually on March 25. If that day falls during Holy Week, the feast is celebrated after Easter.

What's *the* Word?

"Hear, O Israel! The Lord is our God, the Lord alone! Therefore, you shall love the Lord, your God, with all your heart, and with all your soul, and with all your strength. Take to heart these words which I enjoin on you today. Drill them into your children. Speak of them at home and abroad, whether you are busy or at rest." (Deuteronomy 6:4–7)

- Circle the phrase that answers: Who shall we love?

- Underline the phrases that tell how you should love God.

DISCIPLE

Pray
Learn
Celebrate
Share
Choose
Live

More to Explore

Keeping the First Commandment means that we put God first in our lives. Some Catholic men and women put God first in their lives by living in communities of prayer. They live the *monastic life*. Each monastic community lives in a place called a monastery. These men and women give their lives to God in prayer for the world. They work to support themselves in various ways, such as farming or making bread to sell. All that they do is offered to God in prayer.

↳ DISCIPLE CHALLENGE

- How do people who live in monasteries put God first in their lives?

  _____

- Anything we do can be offered to God in prayer. What can you offer to God in prayer?

  _____

Pray Today

My God, I believe in you,
I trust you, I love you.

Make it Happen

The Church teaches that we live out the First Commandment when we honor God in prayer and worship. What prayers of praise and thanksgiving can you say to express your love of God?

_____

_____

_____

Take Home

The Angelus is a prayer that is prayed three times a day: 6 A.M., 12 NOON, and 6 P.M. This prayer recalls the events of the Annunciation. Pray this part of The Angelus with your family.

The angel spoke God's message to Mary, and she conceived of the Holy Spirit.

Hail Mary . . .

"I am the lowly servant of the Lord: let it be done to me according to your word."

Hail Mary . . .

CHAPTER TEST

Circle the correct answer.

1. Giving worship to a creature or thing instead of God is _____.

   lying   idolatry   laziness

2. Our greatest act of love and worship is _____.

   the Mass   the Shema   idolatry

3. The Israelites worshiped the _____.

   sun   moon   one true God

4. Giving God thanks and praise is _____.

   worship   love   idolatry

Match each phrase on the left with its definition on the right.

5. _____ to set up a false god

6. _____ to trust in God

7. _____ to pray to God

8. _____ to worship God

   a. to believe in God's love for us

   b. to give God thanks and praise

   c. to worship a person or thing instead of God

   d. to listen and talk to God with our minds and hearts

Answer the following.

9. Write one thing Mary did to show that she trusted God completely.

   _____

10. Write two ways that you can live out the First Commandment.

   _____

   _____

The Second Commandment

WE GATHER

✝ **Leader:** "Glory in his holy name; rejoice, O hearts that seek the LORD!" (Psalm 105:3)

All: "Glory . . . ." (as above)

Leader: Let us pray.
Loving God, we glory in your name as we call you Father.
We glory in the name of Jesus.
We glory in the name of the Holy Spirit.
O God, we glory in your name!

All: "Glory . . . ."

Leader: Glory to the Father and to the Son, and to the Holy Spirit:

All: As it was in the beginning, is now, and will be for ever.
Amen.

🎵 **Lord, I Lift Your Name on High**

Lord, I lift your name on high.
Lord, I love to sing your praises.
I'm so glad you're in my life.
I'm so glad you came to save us.
You came from heaven to earth to show the way.
From the earth to the cross, my debt to pay.
From the cross to the grave, from the grave to the sky;
Lord, I lift your name on high.
Lord, I lift your name on high.

☀ Do you or a family member or friend have a special nickname? Why do we give special names to people?

WE BELIEVE

God's name is holy.

Because of his love God revealed himself to his people. When God made himself known to Moses, Moses asked his name. God answered, "I am who am" (Exodus 3:14). The Hebrew letters of God's response form the name Yahweh.

The Israelites knew that God was holy. They understood that his name was holy, too. Out of respect for God's holiness, the Israelites did not say the name Yahweh aloud. Instead they called upon God as Lord. They praised the name of the Lord often. For instance, the Israelites prayed,
"From the rising of the sun to its setting
   let the name of the LORD be praised"
(Psalm 113:3).

The Israelites wrote many psalms like this one to the Lord. A **psalm** is a song of praise to honor the Lord. The Book of Psalms is in the Old Testament.

Like the Israelites, we believe that God's name is holy. The Second Commandment is, "You shall not take the name of the LORD your God in vain." To take God's name in vain means to use it in a disrespectful or unnecessary way. The Second Commandment reminds us that God is holy and so is his name. It reminds us to honor God and his name.

What are some ways we can praise God and his holy name?

We respect God's name.

Respecting God's name and the name of Jesus is a sign of the respect we owe to God. Each time that we use God's name, we are calling on the all-powerful God. We call on God by using one of his many titles. These titles come from ways that God works in our lives today. They come from ways God has acted in the lives of his people.

As Christians, we use many titles of God to call upon the Three Persons of the Blessed Trinity. For instance, when we pray the Sign of the Cross we say, "In the name of the Father, and of the Son, and of the Holy Spirit." We are calling upon the Blessed Trinity with reverence. The word **reverence** means honor, love, and respect.

The Second Commandment teaches us to honor and respect God's name and the name of Jesus. The Second Commandment also reminds us to honor and respect the names of Mary and all the saints. Because of the lives they lived, these holy people are with God forever.

As Catholics...

In the Sacrament of Baptism, we are baptized in the name of the Father, and of the Son, and of the Holy Spirit. We are blessed in the name of the Blessed Trinity. We receive the gift of grace for the first time.

At Baptism we may receive a Christian name as a sign of new life. This name may honor a saint or a Christian quality such as faith, hope, or charity. It may also be a name from the Bible.

Find out why you were given your name.

Here are some titles we use to call on God.

Lord

Father

Merciful God

God of wisdom and love

God of hope and light

Almighty, ever-living God

Creator

Holy One

With a partner add to this list of titles. Include titles you have heard before, those you can find in the Bible, and titles that you feel describe God.

Each day this week call on God using one of his many titles. Ask God to be with you as you pray, work, and play.

Titles for God

_____

_____

_____

_____

Key Words

psalm (p. 261)

reverence (p. 261)

We call upon God's name.

We can use God's name to

- praise him and give him our love and respect

- call upon him and ask him to be with us and others

- ask him to forgive us when we have turned away from him

- thank him for being with us and giving us all that we need

- bless ourselves and others. To **bless** is to dedicate someone or something to God or to make something holy in God's name.

When we use God's name in these ways, we obey the Second Commandment.

We also respect God's name when we use it to show that we are truthful. For example, when we take an oath, we place our hand on a Bible and call on God. We call on God to witness that we are speaking the truth. If what we are saying is not true, then we are using God's name in vain.

Sometimes in anger people may use God's name to curse, or call harm on, others. When they do this, they are using God's name in vain.

To follow the Second Commandment, we must always honor God's name. Jesus honored God's name as holy. He taught us to pray, "Father, hallowed be your name" (Luke 11:2). Each time we

call on God with love and respect or use his name in truth, we keep his name holy. Following the Second Commandment also requires us to have a deep respect for all of his children. We should use their names, too, with respect.

In what ways have you used God's name this week? Have you respected God's name and the name of Jesus?

We respect and honor sacred places.

Jesus taught his followers to honor God and to speak respectfully when using God's name. But he also taught his followers to honor places that are dedicated to God. These places are sacred. **Sacred** is another word for holy.

Key Words

bless (p. 259)
sacred (p. 261)

94

The following story is about respecting and honoring the house of God.

The Temple in Jerusalem was a very holy place. Once Jesus saw that some people were selling and buying things in a certain part of the Temple. Jesus then "overturned the tables of the money changers and the seats of those who were selling doves." Jesus used the words of a prophet, saying, "'My house shall be a house of prayer,' but you are making it a den of thieves" (Matthew 21:12, 13).

Jesus was angry at the disrespect people were showing toward God's holy place. We are called to respect sacred places. The Second Commandment reminds us that places where we worship God and honor his name are holy, too.

How can you show respect for holy places?

WE RESPOND

Imagine that you are writing and designing a public service announcement that teaches people to use God's name with respect.

Use this storyboard below to plan your announcement.

PROJECT

Show What *you* Know

In the letter box, circle the answers to the clues. Look forward, backward, up, down, and diagonally.

1. A song of praise to honor the Lord

2. Honor, love, and respect

3. Another word for holy

4. Dedicate someone or something to God or make something holy in God's name

5. To call on God to witness that we are speaking the truth

6. Three titles for God

D	R	R	O	T	A	E	R	C	E
R	S	P	P	S	A	L	M	E	C
O	T	G	S	O	H	T	A	O	D
L	R	E	V	E	R	E	N	C	E
A	L	M	I	G	H	T	Y	S	N
B	A	D	E	R	C	A	S	M	E

Copy the left over letters in order. You will find a hidden message.

Hidden message: ___ ___ ___ ___ ___ ___

___ ___ ___ , ___ ___ ___ ___ ___

Pray Today

As Christians we have a special prayer called the Jesus Prayer. Begin by closing your eyes and being still. Then, as you breathe in, say very quietly, "Jesus." As you breathe out, say, "Savior," or "Peace" or another short word that reminds you of Jesus. Pray the Jesus Prayer now.

Question Corner

Take a survey. Ask five or more friends when they will ask for God's blessing this week. Write your findings here.

_____

_____

_____

_____

DISCIPLE

Pray
Learn
Celebrate
Share
Choose
Live

What's the Word?

"Praise the LORD, all you nations!
Give glory, all you peoples!
The LORD's love for us is strong;
the LORD is faithful forever.
Hallelujah!" (Psalm 117:1–2)

• What does the psalm writer call upon nations to do?

_____

• How does the psalm writer describe God?

_____

More to Explore

The word *litany* comes from the Greek word for "prayer." A litany is a prayer that is sung or said to ask requests of God. Litanies show reverence for God by using many different titles or descriptions that honor God.

↳ **DISCIPLE CHALLENGE**

• Underline the sentence that tells what a litany is.

• How do litanies show reverence for God?

_____

_____

_____

Find a litany that you can pray with your family.

Now, pass it on!

Take Home

Make a blessing banner to put up in your home. It might say, "Bless this Home," or "Bless this Family." Use it as a reminder to keep the Second Commandment.

CHAPTER TEST

Circle the correct answer.

1. _____ is another word for holy.

   Psalm   Sacred   Vain

2. We _____ God, his name, and the places where we worship him.

   honor   curse   disrespect

3. The word _____ means honor, love, and respect.

   magic   *reverence*   *cursing*

4. We believe that God's name is _____.

   a psalm   holy   an oath

Complete the following.

5. When Moses asked God what his name was, God answered

   _____.

6. Taking God's name in vain means

   _____.

7. We honor and respect the names of Mary and all of the saints because

   _____.

8. One way that we follow the Second Commandment is

   _____.

9. To bless means

   _____.

10. One way we show respect for sacred places is

   _____.

WE GATHER

✝ **Leader:** Let us sing together.

🎵 **Open Our Hearts**

God, we come to worship you:

Refrain:
Open our hearts to listen to you.
Open our hearts to listen to you.

God, you made us, we are yours:
(Refrain)

God, your love is always true:
(Refrain)

Faithful God, we trust in you:
(Refrain)

Leader: Let us pray. God the Holy Spirit, keep our hearts open to love and worship God. Help us to make the time in our lives to praise our loving and generous God.

All: Amen.

☀ Think of a time you spent a day doing something special with someone. What made the day special? What made it different from other days?

WE BELIEVE

God gave us a special day to rest and to worship him.

In six days God created the heavens, the earth, and all that is in them. "He rested on the seventh day from all the work he had undertaken. So God blessed the seventh day and made it holy." (Genesis 2:2–3)

The Israelites set apart the seventh day of the week, known today as Saturday, to rest and to honor God in a special way. They kept this day as their **Sabbath**.

Sabbath is a Hebrew word that means "rest." It is written in the book of Exodus that God told his people: "Remember to keep holy the sabbath day" (Exodus 20:8).

On the Sabbath day the Israelites praised God for creation. They thanked God for freeing them from slavery in Egypt. They remembered the covenant God made with them. They thought about the ways they were following God's law.

Like the Israelites and later the Jews, Christians have a day dedicated to God. However, we celebrate our holy day on the first day of the week, Sunday. It was on the first day of the week that Christ rose from the dead. This is why we call Sunday the Lord's Day.

In the Third Commandment we are told, "Remember to keep holy the Lord's Day." Every Sunday we gather to celebrate that Jesus died and rose to save us. We rest from any work or activities that keep us from making the Lord's Day holy.

Why is it important to set aside time for God? How can you make this Sunday a day to honor God?

We keep the Lord's Day holy by participating in Sunday Mass.

In the Gospels we read that Jesus went to the synagogue on the Sabbath. The **synagogue** is the gathering place where Jewish People pray and learn about God. Jesus kept the Sabbath holy by praying and by doing good things for others. He also spent time with his family and friends on the Sabbath.

The first Christians continued to set apart a day for rest and for worship of God. They came together in their homes to celebrate the Lord's Day. On this day, "They devoted themselves to the teaching of the apostles and to the communal life, to the breaking of the bread and to the prayers" (Acts of the Apostles 2:42).

A Jewish community worshiping in the synagogue on the Sabbath

Priests leading the assembly at Sunday Mass

Each time that we participate in Mass we are obeying the words of Jesus: "Do this in memory of me" (Luke 22:19). As Catholics we must participate in Mass on Sundays. In many parishes this Mass is celebrated on Saturday evenings, too.

We also must participate in Mass on holy days of obligation. A **holy day of obligation** is a day set apart to celebrate a special event in the life of Jesus, Mary, or the saints.

We, too, come together to celebrate the Lord's Day. On Sundays we gather as a Church community for the celebration of the Mass. Participating in the Mass is the most important thing that we do to keep the Lord's Day holy. This is because the Eucharist is at the very center of our life and worship.

Holy Days of Obligation in the United States

Solemnity of Mary, Mother of God
(January 1)

Ascension
(when celebrated on Thursday during the Easter season)*

Assumption of Mary
(August 15)

All Saints' Day
(November 1)

Immaculate Conception
(December 8)

Christmas
(December 25)

*(Some dioceses celebrate the Ascension on the following Sunday.)

 It is important that every person take part in the Mass. In what ways can you and your family be involved in the celebration of Mass?

_____

_____

_____

Key Words

Sabbath (p. 261)

synagogue (p. 261)

holy day of obligation (p. 260)

The Lord's Day is a day for rest and relaxation.

Doing things that we enjoy helps us to rest and relax. Doing things we enjoy together strengthens our families and friendships. Rest and relaxation are an important part of following the Third Commandment. Relaxing can help us to be more aware of God's presence and goodness.

The Lord's Day is a good time to share the gifts God has given us. We can share a meal with our family and enjoy one another's company. We can spend time reading from the Bible and praying as a family. We can get together with friends. We can take time to visit people who are sick or unable to leave their homes. We can take part in parish activities to help others.

All the things that we do should bring us closer to God and remind us that God has given us many gifts. Being thankful brings us closer to God and to one another. In this way we keep the Lord's Day holy all day long.

Ask your family members if they know of other names for the Lord's Day.

Discuss some things you like to do. Would it be good to do these things on Sunday? Why or why not?

We keep the Lord's Day holy by caring for the needs of others.

Doing good things for others in Jesus' name helps us to make Sunday holy. The Works of Mercy are ways we can care for the needs of others.

People have different kinds of needs. We can care for the physical needs of people. *Corporal* means "of the body." The things that we do to care for the physical needs of others are the **Corporal Works of Mercy**.

Corporal Works of Mercy

Feed the hungry.

Give drink to the thirsty.

Clothe the naked.

Visit the imprisoned.

Shelter the homeless.

Visit the sick.

Bury the dead.

As Catholics...

The Church has different names for the Lord's Day. The Lord's Day has been called the *First Day*. This is because Jesus rose from the dead on the first day of the week. Another name for the Lord's Day is the *Day of Light*. We know that God created light and that Jesus is the Light of the World. Because of Jesus we can see and know God's love.

We can care for the spiritual needs of people. *Spiritual* means "of the spirit." The things that we do to care for the minds, hearts, and souls of others are the **Spiritual Works of Mercy**.

Key Words

Corporal Works of Mercy (p. 259)

Spiritual Works of Mercy (p. 261)

Spiritual Works of Mercy

Admonish the sinner.
(Give correction to those who need it.)

Instruct the ignorant.
(Share our knowledge with others.)

Counsel the doubtful.
(Give advice to those who need it.)

Comfort the sorrowful.
(Comfort those who suffer.)

Bear wrongs patiently.
(Be patient with others.)

Forgive all injuries.
(Forgive those who hurt us.)

Pray for the living and the dead.

WE RESPOND

Read the first column below. Use the second column to explain how each activity can help people to keep the Lord's Day holy. Share your answers. Circle the activities that are Works of Mercy.

Participating in Mass	
Playing sports	
Shopping at the mall	
Going to the movies	
Visiting a sick friend	
Sharing the family meal	
Reading the Bible	

Thank God for giving us a special time to rest and to praise him.

PROJECT

Show What *you* Know

Use the  Key Words to complete the crossword puzzle.

Down

1. Gathering place where Jewish People pray and learn about God

2. A day of rest set apart to honor God in a special way

3. Works of Mercy that care for the physical needs of others

Across

4. A holy day of _____ is set apart to celebrate a special event in the life of Jesus, Mary, or the saints.

5. Works of Mercy that care for the minds, hearts, and souls of others

Celebrate!

What is the next holy day of obligation in this liturgical year?

_____

What are the ways your parish will be celebrating this day?

_____

_____

_____

DISCIPLE

More to Explore

Young people are encouraged to participate at Mass as altar servers. They are trained to assist the priest at the celebration of the Mass. They often lead the assembly in procession with the cross, and lighted altar candles. Altar servers behave in a reverent way.

DISCIPLE CHALLENGE

- This week, be aware of the ways the altar servers participate at Mass.

- What are some ways you will participate at Mass this week?

_____

_____

What's the Word?

Jesus said, "For I was hungry and you gave me food, I was thirsty and you gave me drink, a stranger and you welcomed me, naked and you clothed me, ill and you cared for me, in prison and you visited me"
(Matthew 25:35–36).

DISCIPLE CHALLENGE

- Jesus described things we should do to care for the physical needs of others. What do we call these actions?

_____

- What ways does your parish live out these Works of Mercy?

_____

_____

Take Home

One way to keep the Lord's Day holy is to be on time for Mass. List three things you can you do to help get yourself ready on time.

_____

_____

_____

Talk with your family about your suggestions and other ways to arrive for Mass without feeling rushed.

105

CHAPTER TEST

Write True or False for the following sentences.
Then change the false sentences to make them true.

1. _____ Catholics must participate in Mass on Sundays and holy days of obligation.

   _____

2. _____ A synagogue is the gathering place where Jewish People pray.

   _____

3. _____ Sunday is like any other day of the week.

   _____

4. _____ Spending time with our families is not an important part of keeping the Lord's Day holy.

   _____

Complete the following.

5. The Third Commandment tells us to

   _____.

6. We celebrate Sunday as the Lord's Day because

   _____.

7–8. Name two Corporal Works of Mercy.

   _____

   _____

9–10. Name two Spiritual Works of Mercy.

   _____

   _____

WE GATHER

✝ **Leader:** A reading from the first Letter of Saint Paul to the Corinthians

"For I received from the Lord what I also handed on to you, that the Lord Jesus, on the night he was handed over, took bread, and, after he had given thanks, broke it and said, 'This is my body that is for you. Do this in remembrance of me.' In the same way also the cup, after supper, saying, 'This cup is the new covenant in my blood. Do this, as often as you drink it, in remembrance of me.' For as often as you eat this bread and drink the cup, you proclaim the death of the Lord until he comes."

(1 Corinthians 11:23–26)

The word of the Lord.

All: Thanks be to God.

🎵 **Ven al Banquete/ Come to the Feast**

Ven, ven al banquete.
Ven a la fiesta de Dios.
Here the hungry find plenty,
here the thirsty shall drink.
Ven a la cena de Cristo,
come to the feast.

☀ What are some things you are thankful for? In what ways do you show others your thanks?

The Introductory Rites unite us and prepare us for worship.

When we participate in the Eucharist, we thank God for creating the world, for saving us from sin, and for making us a holy people. The celebration of the Eucharist is also called the **Mass**. The Mass has four parts: the Introductory Rites, the Liturgy of the Word, the Liturgy of the Eucharist, and the Concluding Rites.

The Introductory Rites unite us as the Body of Christ. They also prepare us to hear God's Word and to celebrate the Eucharist.

The Church is the Body of Christ on earth. Jesus is the head of the Body, and he is with us always. Like the human body, the Church has many parts, or members. Each member is important. Different members have different gifts and talents. All the members are united by the same love for and belief in Jesus Christ.

It is the Body of Christ that gathers for the celebration of the Mass. This community of people gathered to worship in the name of Jesus Christ is called the **assembly**. We are part of the assembly. The assembly offers thanks and praise to God throughout the Mass.

You are a part of the Body of Christ. What gifts and talents will you share with the Church?

During the Liturgy of the Word, we hear the Word of God.

After the Introductory Rites, the Liturgy of the Word begins. The **Liturgy of the Word** is the part of the Mass when we listen and respond to God's Word. We grow in faith as we hear about God's great love. We hear how God is present among us today.

On Sundays and holy days of obligation, there are three readings. The first two readings are read from a special book called the Lectionary. The first reading is usually from the Old Testament. We hear about God's love and mercy for his people. After the first reading we sit in silence. Then we pray by singing a psalm. The second reading is from the New Testament. It is usually from a letter written by one of Jesus' first disciples. We are encouraged to live together as followers of Jesus.

Before the third reading, we stand to show that we are ready to listen to the Good News of Jesus Christ. The third reading, always from one of the four Gospels of the New Testament, is read from the *Book of the Gospels*. The deacon or priest proclaims this reading. We hear about the words and actions of Jesus during his ministry. We hear about the ways Jesus wants his disciples to live.

Then the priest or deacon gives a homily. The **homily** is a talk that helps us to understand the readings and to grow as faithful followers of Jesus.

At Mass we state what we believe by saying the Creed. We then remember the needs of all God's People by praying the Prayer of the Faithful. We pray for the Church and its leaders. We pray for those who are in need, those who are sick, and those who have died.

With a group act out one story about Jesus and his work. Write one way this story applies to your life.

_____

_____

The Bible is the Word of God. It is also called Sacred Scripture. This is because God the Holy Spirit guided the human writers of the Bible. They wrote what God wanted to share with us.

God speaks to us through the words of the Bible. The Bible is God's living Word to us. It is a record of the ways God has acted in the lives of his people. It is also about the ways we are called to live and respond to God. The Bible helps us to know and understand that God is with us today.

Plan a time this week to read from the Bible with your family.

Key Words

Mass (p. 260)

assembly (p. 259)

Liturgy of the Word (p. 260)

homily (p. 260)

During the Liturgy of the Eucharist, we offer gifts of bread and wine and receive the Body and Blood of Jesus Christ.

In the Liturgy of the Word, we are nourished as we listen to God's living Word. In the Liturgy of the Eucharist, we are nourished by the Body and Blood of Christ. The **Liturgy of the Eucharist** is the part of the Mass in which the Death and Resurrection of Christ are made present again; our gifts of bread and wine become the Body and Blood of Christ, which we receive in Holy Communion.

Here is what happens during the Liturgy of the Eucharist:

- Members of the assembly bring forward gifts of bread and wine. The gifts represent all the blessings God has given to us. Money and other offerings are also brought forward. This shows our concern for our parish and for those in need.

- The priest prays the Eucharistic Prayer in our name. The **Eucharistic Prayer** is the Church's greatest prayer of praise and thanksgiving to God.

- We pray the Lord's Prayer together. We call on God the Father to give us the things we need and to forgive us. As a sign of our love and unity, we offer one another a sign of peace. The priest then breaks the Host while we pray the "Lamb of God."

- The assembly comes forward to receive Holy Communion. We sing to show our joy and thankfulness. After we receive Holy Communion, we pray quietly. Holy Communion makes the life of God in us stronger. It strengthens us to be Christ to one another.

In the Eucharistic Prayer:

- We honor God for all he has done. We join with the angels to give God praise.

- The priest asks the Holy Spirit to come upon our gifts of bread and wine and make them holy. Then he says and does what Jesus said and did at the Last Supper. The priest takes the bread and says, "FOR THIS IS MY BODY." Taking the cup of wine, the priest says, "FOR THIS IS THE CHALICE OF MY BLOOD." This part of the Eucharistic Prayer is called the **Consecration**. By the power of the Holy Spirit and through the words and actions of the priest, the bread and wine become the Body and Blood of Christ. Jesus is truly present in the Eucharist. This is called the *Real Presence*.

- We proclaim the mystery of faith by calling to mind the Death, Resurrection, and coming of the risen Lord in glory.

- We pray that the Holy Spirit will unite the Church in Heaven and on earth. The Eucharistic Prayer ends with our great Amen. We are saying yes to the prayer the priest has prayed in our name.

 What do we see and do during the Liturgy of the Eucharist? Why?

In the Concluding Rites we are sent to live as disciples of Jesus.

The final part of the Mass is the Concluding Rites. The priest blesses us in God's name. We answer, "Amen." Then the deacon or priest dismisses us. He may say, "Go and announce the Gospel of the Lord." We usually sing a final hymn before we leave the church.

We leave the Eucharist filled with grace and peace. We have been nourished by God's Word and by the Body and Blood of Christ. We have been united with Christ and with one another. We have been strengthened to perform Works of Mercy for others. We try to be signs of God's love and presence in the world.

We act as disciples of Jesus. We share our gifts, our talents, and our time with others. We work for peace and justice in our homes, our schools, and our neighborhoods.

WE RESPOND

 Illustrate a way you will love and serve God this week.

Key Words

Liturgy of the Eucharist (p. 260)

Eucharistic Prayer (p. 259)

Consecration (p. 259)

PROJECT

Pray
Learn
Celebrate
Share
Choose
Live

Show What *you* Know

Match the 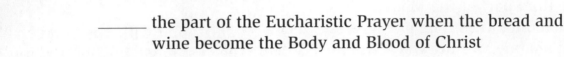 Key Words with their definitions.

1. assembly

_____ the part of the Mass when we listen to God's Word

2. Consecration

_____ the Church's greatest prayer of praise and thanksgiving to God

3. Eucharistic Prayer

_____ the celebration of the Eucharist

4. homily

_____ the part of the Eucharistic Prayer when the bread and wine become the Body and Blood of Christ

5. Liturgy of the Eucharist

_____ talk given by the priest or deacon that helps us understand the readings

6. Liturgy of the Word

_____ community of people gathered to worship in the name of Jesus Christ

7. Mass

_____ the part of the Mass in which the Death and Resurrection of Christ are made present again

Picture This

Draw you and your friends living as disciples of Jesus.

DISCIPLE

Pray
Learn
Celebrate
Share
Choose
Live

Saint Stories

Paschal Baylon worked as a shepherd in the hills of Spain. Paschal entered the religious community of the Franciscans and became a brother. He spent time praying in front of the Most Blessed Sacrament. He wrote letters urging devotion to the Eucharist. He said, "Seek God above all things." He is the patron saint of those devoted to the Eucharist. His feast day is May 17.

↳ DISCIPLE CHALLENGE

- Circle the group for whom Paschal Baylon is the patron saint.
- Underline what he told people to do.

Pray Today

My good Jesus, I thank you with all my heart. How good, how kind you are to me, sweet Jesus! Blessed be Jesus in the most Holy Sacrament. Remain with me, O Lord. Always keep me close to you.

Fast Facts

A special light, called the *sanctuary lamp*, is always kept burning in the church near the tabernacle. This light reminds us that Jesus Christ is present there in the Most Blessed Sacrament.

Take Home

Your family can visit the Most Blessed Sacrament to show your love and devotion to Jesus. Talk with your family about taking time to make a visit to the Most Blessed Sacrament in your church. Tell Jesus of your love, needs, hopes, and thanks.

Circle the correct answer.

1. The part of the Eucharistic Prayer when the bread and wine become the Body and Blood of Christ is called the _____.

   Creed   Consecration   song

2. The _____ offers thanks and praise to God throughout the Mass.

   homily   assembly   Bible

3. The Introductory Rites, the Liturgy of the Word, the Liturgy of the Eucharist, and the Concluding Rites are the four parts of the _____.

   Gloria   Mass   Bible

4. We hear about the words and actions of Jesus during his ministry when the _____ is proclaimed.

   Gospel   psalm   Creed

Write True or False for the following sentences.
Then change the false sentences to make them true.

5. _____ Jesus is truly present in the Eucharist.

_____

_____

6. _____ The Creed and the Prayer of the Faithful are part of the Introductory Rites.

_____

_____

7. _____ God speaks to us through the words of the Bible.

_____

_____

8. _____ The first two readings at Mass are taken from the *Book of the Gospels.*

_____

_____

Write a sentence to answer each question.

9. What is the homily?

_____

10. What is one important thing that happens during the Eucharistic Prayer?

_____

"Come to us, Lord, and bring us peace.
We will rejoice in your presence and
serve you with all our heart."

Communion Rite, Monday, First Week of Advent

SEASONAL
CHAPTER 13

**This chapter prepares us to celebrate
the season of Advent.**

WE GATHER

✝ *Mary, help us to prepare for the coming of Jesus.*

What are some things you anticipate, or look forward to, with excitement?

WE BELIEVE

The season of Advent is a time of preparation. It is a season of joyful hope and anticipation. During the four weeks of Advent we prepare ourselves for the coming of the Lord. In fact, the word *Advent* means "coming."

During the season of Advent, we hope for Christ's coming in the future, and we prepare by being his faithful followers today. We celebrate that Jesus is with us today, and we prepare to celebrate that he first came to us over two thousand years ago in Bethlehem.

We begin Advent by praying for Jesus Christ to come again at the end of time. We know that Jesus will return because he told us that he would. We do not know exactly when Christ will come again. Yet as people of faith, we trust that he will. We do know that Jesus wants us to be ready. He wants us to prepare by living a life that shows that we are his disciples. When Jesus comes again, he will comfort his people: "He will wipe every tear from their eyes" (Revelation 21:4). He will come to bring us into his kingdom of peace, joy, and love. We get ready by following the commandments and following Jesus' teachings. We prepare our hearts.

In Advent we celebrate more than the future coming of Jesus. We also celebrate his coming in our world and his presence in the world today. When we pray, "Come, Lord Jesus" with the Church during Advent, we pray knowing that Jesus is always with us. Jesus tells us, "For where two or three are gathered together in my name, there am I in the midst of them" (Matthew 18:20). Jesus comes to us every day in the celebration of the Eucharist, in all the sacraments, and in the love we have for one another.

In our world today many people are hungry or homeless. Many people are suffering from war and disease. When we pray, "Come, Lord Jesus," we pray that Jesus will come to those who need him most, and to us that we may share his love with others.

As Advent comes to an end, we focus our waiting and preparing on Jesus' first coming. We prepare as Mary prepared for the birth of her Son. We share her anticipation as we wait for the coming of the Savior.

 During Advent in what ways do we prepare for and celebrate the coming of Christ? In groups plan a play about the meaning of Advent. Produce the play for the class.

Bishop kneels before Virgin Mary's image on Saint Juan Diego's cloak.

During the season of Advent we have feast days that help us prepare for Christ's coming. Two of these feasts are related. On December 12 we honor Mary as Our Lady of Guadalupe, the patroness of the Americas. On December 9 we remember Saint Juan Diego, to whom Our Lady of Guadalupe appeared.

Juan Diego was a farm worker who lived outside of a city known today as Mexico City. There were not many Christians in this area, but Juan Diego believed in Christ. Every day he walked fifteen miles to participate in Mass. On his way to Mass the morning of December 9, 1531, Juan passed Tepeyac Hill. He heard music and saw a glowing cloud. When he got to the top of the hill, a young woman dressed like an Aztec princess was there. She spoke to Juan in his own language and said that she was the Virgin Mary. She asked that a church be built on the hill so that she could give her love, compassion, and help to the people.

Juan went to the bishop with this news. The bishop kindly listened to Juan, but could not believe that this really happened. Then on December 12 the Virgin Mary appeared to Juan again as the Aztec Lady. She told him to climb the hill where they had met. When he did, Juan found flowers growing in the frozen soil. They were roses which did not even grow in Mexico. He gathered them in his cloak and went at once to the bishop. When Juan opened his cloak the flowers fell to the ground. And on the inside of Juan's cloak was a glowing image of the Lady. She became known as Our Lady of Guadalupe.

Soon after, a church was built on this hill where our Lady had appeared. Since that time a special devotion to Mary as Our Lady of Guadalupe has grown, and millions of Native Mexicans have been baptized as followers of her son, Jesus Christ.

WE RESPOND

We learn from Our Lady of Guadalupe that we need to appreciate the culture of those to whom we bring the Good News. If it were not for Mary, millions of people may not have known the love of Christ. We, too, need to understand people so that we can help them to understand and know Christ. What is one way you can follow Mary's example this week?

✝ We Respond in Prayer

🎵 **Somos el Cuerpo de Cristo/**
   We Are the Body of Christ

Refrain: Somos el cuerpo de Cristo.
　　　　We are the body of Christ.
　　　　Hemos oído el llamado;
　　　　We've answered yes to the call of the Lord.
　　　　Somos el cuerpo de Cristo.
　　　　We are the body of Christ.
　　　　Traemos su santo mensaje.
　　　　We come to bring the good news to the world.

Dios viene al mundo a través do nosotros.
Somos el cuerpo de Cristo.
God is revealed when we love one another.
We are the body of Christ. (Refrain)

Reader: A reading from the Gospel of Luke.
　"My soul proclaims the greatness of the Lord;
　　my spirit rejoices in God my savior.
　For he has looked upon his handmaid's lowliness;
　　behold, from now on will all ages call me blessed.
　The Mighty One has done great things for me,
　　and holy is his name." (Luke 1:46–49)

The Gospel of the Lord.

All: Praise to you, Lord Jesus Christ.

Leader: Let us pray this litany together. Our
　response after each title for Mary is, "Pray for us."

Reader: Holy Mother of God
　Mother of Christ
　Mother of the Church
　Cause of our joy
　Comfort of the troubled
　Queen of peace
　Our Lady of Guadalupe

PROJECT DISCIPLE

Pray
Learn
Celebrate
Share
Choose
Live

Show What *you* Know

Write a paragraph to tell others about Advent.

More *to* Explore

An Advent wreath is a circle of small evergreen branches with four candles. One candle is lighted during each of the four weeks of Advent. Each part of the Advent wreath has a special meaning: evergreen—life; wreath's circle—eternity of God; four candles—four weeks of Advent; lighting the wreath—waiting for the Lord's coming; light—Jesus Christ, the Light of the World.

↳ **DISCIPLE CHALLENGE** Write a prayer for each week of Advent.

Week 1: _____

Week 2: _____

Week 3: _____

Week 4: _____

Take Home

Prepare for the coming of the Lord with your family. Make an Advent wreath, and pray this Advent wreath blessing:

Lord God,

Let your blessing come upon us as we light the candles of this wreath.

May the wreath and its light be a sign of Christ's promise to bring us salvation.

May he come quickly and not delay. We ask this through Christ our Lord. Amen.

Then during each week of Advent, pray the prayer you wrote for that week.

"All the ends of the earth
have seen the saving power of God."

Responsorial Psalm, Christmas Mass During the Day

SEASONAL

This chapter addresses the entire
Christmas season.

CHAPTER 14

During the Christmas season we celebrate the Son of God's coming into the world.

WE GATHER

✝ *You came that we might have the fullness of life.*

Name some countries in different parts of the world. What are some things people in different parts of the world have in common?

WE BELIEVE

Over two thousand years ago Jesus was born in Bethlehem of Judea. But his mission went far beyond that small town in a small country. The Son of God lived among us so that the whole world could know his Father's love. He came for everyone, and he lived for everyone. Jesus Christ died and rose to new life for all people.

During the Christmas season, we celebrate the wonderful event of the Incarnation: that God the Son, the Second Person of the Blessed Trinity, became man. We celebrate that Jesus came to be the light for all nations.

One feast during the season of Christmas, the Feast of the Epiphany, reminds us of this in a special way. We celebrate Jesus' *Epiphany*, or Jesus' showing of himself to the whole world. We read about this event in the Gospel of Matthew.

📖 Matthew 2:1–12

Narrator: When Jesus was born in Bethlehem, magi, or wise men, traveled from the east to find him. They arrived in Jerusalem, saying:

Magi: "Where is the newborn king of the Jews? We saw his star at its rising and have come to do him homage" (Matthew 2:2).

Narrator: When King Herod and the others in Jerusalem heard this, they were very troubled. King Herod asked the magi where the Messiah was born, and they answered:

Magi: "In Bethlehem of Judea, for thus it has been written through the prophet" (Matthew 2:5).

Narrator: The King sent for the magi secretly. He asked them when they had first seen the star. He then said,

King Herod: Go and search for the child. "When you have found him, bring me word, that I too may go and do him homage." (Matthew 2:8)

Narrator: The rising star led the magi to the place where the child was. When they went inside the house they found the child with Mary his mother. They lay down before the child and honored him as a king. "Then they opened their treasures and offered him gifts of gold, frankincense, and myrrh. And having been warned in a dream not to return to Herod, they departed for their country by another way." (Matthew 2:11–12)

During the time of Jesus, many people believed that a new star appeared in the sky whenever a new ruler was born. The magi saw this star from lands far away and came in search of the new king. The magi themselves were not Jewish, yet they wanted to honor Jesus with gifts.

This Epiphany, or showing, of Jesus teaches us that Jesus' coming into the world was important to the whole world. The Good News of Jesus Christ is meant for everyone. We celebrate Christmas Day on December 25 and the Feast of the Epiphany on the second Sunday after that.

The story of the magi's visit has been a part of our Christmas celebrations for centuries. The Gospel of Matthew refers to magi, who were known to be wise men, but does not include how many traveled to honor Jesus. Yet, through the years, the magi have been called the three kings. And over time the kings were given names. Your parish may sing the hymn "We Three Kings" during the Christmas season. This song is actually about the magi.

Throughout history people have also taken an interest in the treasure the magi offered: frankincense, myrrh, and gold. It is said that the:

- frankincense was in honor of Christ being divine because incense is used at the liturgy and for other times of prayer.

- myrrh, a spice used in burials, was in honor of Christ's humanity, because Jesus would die and be buried like all human beings.

- gold was a sign of Christ's kingship because, in Jesus, God's Kingdom is with us.

WE RESPOND

Many people from Spanish-speaking countries have parades to celebrate the Epiphany. Three men dress as kings. They give candy and small presents to the children, just as the magi shared what they had with Jesus.

Some people celebrate the Epiphany with a special cake. A bean is baked into it, and whoever finds the bean is king or queen for the day!

Is there a special way that you can celebrate, too? This week celebrate Jesus' birth and his presence in your life!

_____

_____

Children looking for the bean in the king cake.

✝ We Respond in Prayer

Leader: Let us listen to the words of the Prophet Isaiah.

Reader 1: "Rise up in splendor! Your light has come,
the glory of the Lord shines upon you.
See, darkness covers the earth,
and thick clouds cover the peoples;

Reader 2: But upon you the LORD shines,
and over you appears his glory.
Nations shall walk by your light,
and kings by your shining radiance.

Reader 3: Raise your eyes and look about;
they all gather and come to you:
Your sons come from afar,
and your daughters in the arms of their
nurses." (Isaiah 60:1–4)

The word of the Lord.

All: Thanks be to God.

🎵 Praise Him with Cymbals

In a lowly manger on a dark winter's night,
a star arose in the sky,
and to the Earth it gave a great light,
a bright and glorious sign.

Refrain: O praise him with cymbals,
praise him with dancing,
praise him with glad tambourines.
And praise him with singing,
praise him with clapping,
Jesus is born, Christ the King.

Three wise men came to him,
bearing gifts of frankincense, myrrh and gold;
for the King of kings was born on that night,
as they so wisely foretold. (Refrain)

Celebrate!

During the Christmas season, celebrate the Feast of the Epiphany with your friends and family by acting out the play on pages 122–123.

Reality Check

What are some things you do during the Christmas season?

❏ sing Christmas carols

❏ visit friends and family

❏ go to Mass

❏ visit the parish nativity scene

❏ share gifts with those in need

❏ _____

What's the Word?

"The angel said to them [the shepherds], 'Do not be afraid; for behold, I proclaim to you good news of great joy that will be for all the people. For today in the city of David a savior has been born for you who is Messiah and Lord." (Luke 2:10–11)

↳ **DISCIPLE CHALLENGE**

• Underline the phrase that tells who the Good News is for.

• Circle the three titles for the child born in the city of David.

Take Home

The magi brought gifts of gold, frankincense, and myrrh to the child Jesus. Talk about the "gifts" your family could offer Jesus today.

UNIT TEST

Choose a word from the box to complete each sentence.

1. Jesus lived his life according to the _____ God made with his people.

2. To take God's name in _____ is to use it in a disrespectful or unnecessary way.

3. To give God thanks and praise is to _____ him.

4. It is an act of _____ to put someone or something before God.

5. When we show honor, love, and respect to God, we are showing him _____.

6. To _____ something or someone is to dedicate that thing or that person to God.

7. Feeding the hungry and caring for the sick are _____ Works of Mercy.

8. Comforting the suffering and forgiving those who hurt us are _____ Works of Mercy.

9. The celebration of the _____ is the most important way we keep the Lord's Day.

10. On the Lord's Day we gather to celebrate that _____ died and rose to save us.

bless
Jesus
Corporal
vain
Eucharist
idolatry
covenant
reverence
Spiritual
worship

continued on next page **127**

Write the letter of the Scripture verse that matches each of the following.

11. _____ the Shema

    a. "As I have loved you, so you also should love one another." (John 13:34)

12. _____ the Great Commandment

    b. "I, the LORD, am your God. . . . You shall not have other gods besides me." (Exodus 20:2, 3)

13. _____ the New Commandment

    c. "You shall love the Lord, your God, with all your heart, with all your soul, and with all your mind. You shall love your neighbor as yourself." (Matthew 22:37, 39)

14. _____ the First Commandment

    d. "Hear, O Israel! The LORD is our God, the LORD alone!" (Deuteronomy 6:4)

15. _____ the Second Commandment

    e. "Remember to keep holy the sabbath day." (Exodus 20:8)

16. _____ the Third Commandment

    f. "You shall not take the name of the LORD, your God, in vain." (Exodus 20:7)

Write your answers to the questions on a separate sheet of paper.

17–18. God calls us to respect the human dignity of all people. What can a fourth grader do to show respect for basic human rights?

19–20. What are some ways you can keep Sunday holy?

The Commandments Help Us to Love Others

Seasonal Chapters

In Unit 3 your child will grow as a disciple of Jesus by:

- loving and respecting our families and people in authority
- promoting respect for all life and the rights of all people
- appreciating the ability to show love to others, and living the virtue of chastity
- acting justly toward others, and sharing the goods of God's creation
- witnessing to the truth of our faith, and speaking truth to others.

Saint Stories

Blessed Kateri Tekakwitha is the patron of the environment and ecology. We can follow her example as we live out the Seventh Commandment. Bishop Brzana of Ogdensburg, New York, wrote, "Kateri was a child of nature. Her sainthood will raise the minds and hearts of those who love nature and work in ecology." Kateri is the first Native American to be declared Blessed. Her feast day is July 14.

Pray Today

The Sixth Commandment reminds us of the sacredness of friendship, love, and marriage. Encourage family members to name friends for whom they want to pray, and as a family, pray together for them. Then invite each family member to name a married couple, and as a family, pray together for them. How can your family strengthen friendships and support married couples in their love?

Reality Check

"The family should live in such a way that its members learn to care and take responsibility for the young, the old, the sick, the handicapped and the poor."
(*Catechism of the Catholic Church*, 2208)

Picture This

Look at the photo on page 134. Talk about ways this firefighter helps others. Also talk about how your family can show respect and obey the people who are in roles of service and authority. Tell your child about the people in authority whom you obey and respect—a boss, a professor, etc. Pray together for all parents and others in authority.

What Would you do?

As a family, imagine that you are asked to talk with other families about the ways you care for life—your own and the lives of others—as the Fifth Commandment requires. Make an outline of some of the main points.

_____

_____

Take Home

Be ready for this unit's Take Home:

Chapter 15: Praying to the Holy Family

Chapter 16: Respecting the gift of life

Chapter 17: Rating television shows

Chapter 18: Being stewards of creation

Chapter 19: Living out the Eighth Commandment

The Fourth Commandment

WE GATHER

✝ **Leader:** In the Gospel of Luke, we read about a journey that Jesus, Mary, and Joseph made to the Temple in Jerusalem. When it was time to leave, Mary thought Jesus was with Joseph. Joseph thought Jesus was with Mary. They left Jerusalem without him! For a whole day, they did not realize that he was not with the group. When they did, they went back to look for him. This is where we begin our reading.

Reader 1: "After three days they found him in the temple, sitting in the midst of the teachers, listening to them and asking them questions, and all who heard him were astounded at his understanding and his answers.

Reader 2: When his parents saw him, they were astonished, and his mother said to him, 'Son, why have you done this to us? Your father and I have been looking for you with great anxiety.'

Reader 3: And he said to them, 'Why were you looking for me? Did you not know that I must be in my Father's house?' But they did not understand what he said to them.

Reader 4: He went down with them and came to Nazareth, and was obedient to them; and his mother kept all these things in her heart.

Reader 5: And Jesus advanced [in] wisdom and age and favor before God and man." (Luke 2:46–52)

Leader: Let us pray. God our Father, you gave your Son a family to help him grow. May we, like Jesus, listen to our parents and obey them, so that we too may grow in wisdom, age, and favor before you and all people. We ask through Jesus Christ, our Lord.

All: Amen.

☀ What are some ways you show love and respect for your family? for people in your neighborhood?

WE BELIEVE
God wants us to love and respect others.

The Ten Commandments remind us of our relationship with God. God is always with us. We respond to God by the ways we live out the commandments. The Ten Commandments help us to know how to love God, ourselves, and others. Following the Ten Commandments gives us the happiness that comes from a relationship with God. Living by the Ten Commandments also helps us to be active members of the Church community.

When we follow the first three commandments, we show our love for God. When we follow the Fourth through the Tenth Commandments, we show love for others. All people are made in God's image. Whenever we respect and honor one another, we honor God.

The Fourth Commandment is: "Honor your father and your mother" (Exodus 20:12).

It teaches us to appreciate and obey our parents, our guardians, and all those who lead and serve us. We value and listen with respect to our parents, guardians, teachers, pastors, bishops, the pope, and all those who help us to see God's will for us. We also obey the laws of our city, state, and nation.

Jesus showed us how to live out the Fourth Commandment. He himself was obedient to his mother, Mary, and his foster father, Joseph. Jesus did the things that God his Father wanted. Jesus showed respect for religious leaders— priests, teachers, and leaders who helped to bring people closer to the Father.

Name one way you have followed the Fourth Commandment today.

As Catholics...

Jesus, Mary, and Joseph are called the Holy Family. Each year on the Sunday after Christmas, the Church celebrates the Feast of the Holy Family. On this day we recall the love that Jesus shared with Mary, Joseph, and his other relatives, and his friends. We thank God for the gift of our own families. We ask God to help all families.

How can you and your family show love for God and one another?

In our families we learn to love God and others.

Jesus, Mary, and Joseph are called the Holy Family. They honored and respected one another. They shared both happy and sad times with their relatives and friends. They worked and prayed together. They honored and loved God.

A family is a community. It may be large or small. It may include parents and grandparents, brothers and sisters, aunts and uncles, and cousins. Family members share love and spend time together. They try to live in peace, helping one another.

Christian families are called to be communities of faith, hope, and love.

Through Baptism the members of every Christian family share the very life of God—the Father, the Son, and the Holy Spirit. As Christian families we can pray and worship together. We try to live so that all people will know the love of God. We help people in need. We share our faith in God and love for one another with all those we meet. In these ways, Christian families spread God's Kingdom here on earth.

Every Christian family is called to be a **domestic Church**, or a "Church in the home." Within our families we learn about and experience work, forgiveness, and discipline. We grow in our faith and ability to choose what is good. We learn to take part in the Church community. We work with other families to help build neighborhoods, parishes, nations, and a better world.

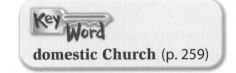

domestic Church (p. 259)

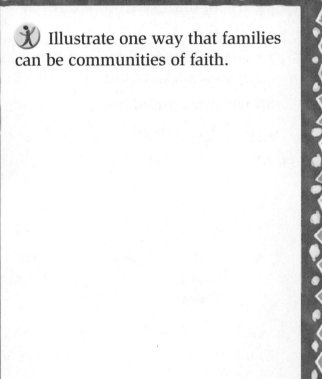

Illustrate one way that families can be communities of faith.

In our families we have the responsibility to love and respect one another.

Parents and guardians have many responsibilities in their families. They try to make sure that their children have the things they need. They care for and protect their children. They teach them about the world in which they live. They help them to learn to work and play with other children.

Catholic parents have a special responsibility to help their children grow in faith. With the Church's help they:

- share their love for and belief in Jesus and his Church

- teach their children about God the Father, Son, and Holy Spirit

- teach their children how to pray and worship with them at Sunday Mass

- help their children to learn the difference between good and evil

- show their children the importance of sharing and caring for the needs of others.

Children have responsibilities to their families, too. An important way to honor our parents and guardians is to obey them. Obedience is doing the just and good things that are asked of us. We keep the Fourth Commandment when we obey and respect our parents, cooperate with them, and appreciate them.

As we grow older, the ways that we show respect and love for our parents

will change. However, the need to honor our parents and guardians will remain.

In what ways do you obey your parents and guardians? How do your parents show respect for their parents?

_____

_____

_____

Citizens and leaders work together for peace.

The Fourth Commandment requires us to respect those who have a responsibility for us, including teachers, Church leaders, and all government leaders. These people are in positions of authority. Those in authority are called to respect the dignity of all people. They are asked to make sure that all people are treated fairly. They are called to work for peace. The only time we should not obey people who are responsible for us is when they ask us to do something that is wrong or unjust.

Learning about and obeying the just laws of our country, state, city, or town is an important way to keep the Fourth Commandment. The laws of our country protect its citizens. We obey these laws and respect the women and men who enforce them.

We want our government to be just and fair, and to do good for the people of our country and the world. So we can write and talk to people who make decisions for our community. We can ask them to work for justice and peace. We can also pray for our leaders and lawmakers, and for the leaders of governments throughout the world.

♫ We Are the Family

Refrain:

We are the fam'ly and we are the home.

We are the mountain where love can be known.

We are the voices and we are the hands for bringing peace to our land.

WE RESPOND

Imagine you are producing a video to teach people about the Fourth Commandment. In a group plan what you would talk about and show on the video. Then act it out.

Pray Learn Celebrate Share Choose Live

PROJECT

Show What *you* Know

Read each clue. Use the letter key to help you to complete the words.

1. What every Christian family is called to be.

Letter Key: H, H, M, C, C, C, S, R, T, D

___ O ___ E ___ ___ I ___   ___ ___ U ___ ___ ___

2. Honor your father and your mother.

Letter Key: M, M, M, N, N, R, F, T, T, D, C, H

___ O U ___ ___ ___   ___ O ___ ___ A ___ ___ ___ E ___ ___

3. What we are called to show people who have responsibility for us.

Letter Key: T, R, S, C, P

___ E ___ ___ E ___ ___

4. Jesus, Mary, and Joseph are called the

Letter Key: L, L, M, Y, Y, H, F

___ O ___ ___   ___ A ___ I ___ ___.

What's *the* Word?

Saint Paul writes, "Children, obey your parents, [in the Lord] for this is right" (Ephesians 6:1).

↳ **DISCIPLE CHALLENGE** In your own words, write Paul's message for today's fourth graders.

_____

_____

_____ **Now, pass it on!**

DISCIPLE

Saint Stories

In 2008, Louis and Zélie Martin, the parents of Saint Thérèse of Lisieux, were named "Blessed" by the Church. This was the first time that parents of a saint were presented for sainthood as a couple. Their family was a domestic Church that serves as a model for all. They taught their children to love God, to pray daily, and to care for the poor and for one another.

↳ DISCIPLE CHALLENGE

- Circle the phrase that describes the family of Louis and Zélie Martin.
- Underline the sentence that tells what Louis and Zélie taught their children.

What Would *you* do?

You and your friends are playing a game after school. An elderly neighbor comes by and tries to start a conversation. Your friends ignore your neighbor and continue the game. You decide to

_____

_____

_____

_____

Take Home

Pray this prayer with your family.

Holy Family of Nazareth, make our family and home more and more like yours, until we are all one family, happy and at peace in our true home with you. Amen.

Copy the prayer. Decorate it to display in your home.

Write True or False for the following sentences.
Then change the false sentences to make them true.

1. _____ The Fourth Commandment is: "Honor your father and your mother."

_____

2. _____ The domestic Church is the parish church.

_____

3. _____ Children honor their parents by obeying them.

_____

4. _____ The Fourth Commandment reminds us to get enough sleep.

_____

Write the letter of the phrase that completes each of the following.

5. _____ The Fourth Commandment

6. _____ Christian families

7. _____ People in authority

8. _____ Obedience

a. are called to respect the dignity of all people.

b. is doing the just and good things that are asked of us.

c. teaches us to honor our parents, and guardians.

d. are called to be communities of faith, hope, and love.

Answer the following.

9. Write one way parents help their children to grow in faith.

_____

10. Write one way Jesus lived out the Fourth Commandment.

_____

The Fifth Commandment

16

WE GATHER

✤ **Leader:** Let us begin by listening to the Word of God.

Reader 1: A reading from the Book of the Prophet Jeremiah

"Before I formed you in the womb
    I knew you,
before you were born
    I dedicated you,
a prophet to the nations
    I appointed you."
(Jeremiah 1:5)

The word of the Lord.

All: Thanks be to God.

Reader 2:
    "I praise you, so wonderfully you
        made me;
    wonderful are your works!"
(Psalm 139:14)

All:
    "I praise you, so wonderfully you
        made me;
    wonderful are your works!"

Reader 3:
    "I praise you, so wonderfully you
        made me;

All: wonderful are your works!"

🎵 **You Are Near**

Refrain:
    Lord, I know you are near,
    standing always at my side.
    You guard me from the foe,
    and you lead me in ways
        everlasting.

    You know my heart and its ways,
    you who formed me
        before I was born,
    in the secret of darkness
        before I saw the sun,
    in my mother's womb.
    (Refrain)

    Marvelous to me are your works;
    how profound are your
        thoughts, my Lord.
    Even if I could count them,
    they number as the stars,
        you would still be there.
    (Refrain)

☀ Who are the people in our neighborhoods and cities who work to protect life? What do they do?

WE BELIEVE
Human life is sacred.

All human life is a gift from God. God shares his life with each and every one of us. Of all God's creation, only we are made to love God and grow in his friendship.

The Fifth Commandment is based on the belief that all life is sacred, created by God. The Fifth Commandment states, "You shall not kill" (Exodus 20:13; Deuteronomy 5:17). To follow this commandment we must respect and protect human life. We must value life in all that we say and do.

During the Sermon on the Mount, Jesus taught about the Fifth Commandment. He said, "You have heard it was said to your ancestors, 'You shall not kill; and whoever kills will be liable to judgment.' But I say to you, whoever is angry with his brother will be liable to judgment" (Matthew 5:21–22).

Jesus asks us to have peace in our hearts, not anger. Anger can lead people to say and do things that hurt the lives of others, and their own lives.

Living out the Fifth Commandment requires us to respect all life and the dignity of all people. **Human dignity** is the value and worth each person has from being created in God's image and likeness. This gift gives us the ability to think, to make choices, and to love. Human dignity makes us someone, not something. It makes us all equal with one another.

Talk about ways people are equal. What can we do to respect all people as made in God's image?

140

The right to life is the most basic human right.

The Fifth Commandment teaches us about the right to life. Each of us has this right from the moment of conception to the moment of natural death. Unfortunately, not all the things that people do value and protect human life.

For example, people are sometimes violent. They act in ways that destroy things or injure others. Violence against people can lead to the disregard for human life. However, because our own life is sacred, we have the right to protect and defend ourselves.

The deliberate killing of an innocent person is a very serious sin. It takes away that person's life.

- Unborn children deserve protection and respect as all people do. They have the right to life.

- Our own lives are a gift from God. A person does not have the right to commit suicide, or to take one's own life.

- People who are sick, disabled, elderly, or dying have the same right to life as all people. They deserve our care and protection.

As Catholics...

Jesus told us not to have anger in our hearts. Anger is a feeling that can lead us to act in harmful ways. However, sometimes anger can lead us to speak out for what is right and help others to change unjust situations. Feelings themselves are not right or wrong. However, the way we deal with or act on our feelings can be.

This week try to think before you act on your feelings.

Key Word

human dignity (p. 260)

Think about the television shows you have seen or computer games you have played lately. Name some ways they showed human life being valued or being harmed.

We respect the gift of life.

God created each of us. We trust that he will continue to give us what we need for life. Jesus taught us to ask God our Father for "our daily bread" (Matthew 6:11). Each time we pray the Our Father, we ask God to provide for us and for others.

When we take care of ourselves and those in need, we show that we are grateful for the gift of life. We show respect for life when we give food to the hungry and care for those who are sick. When we live a healthy life, we show respect for the life we have been given.

Here are some ways we can live the Fifth Commandment.

Take proper care of our bodies.

- Do not take drugs, smoke cigarettes, or drink alcohol.
- Eat a balanced diet and exercise.
- Avoid dangerous activities that can harm us.

Take care of our minds, hearts, and souls.

- Spend time studying and learning.
- Pray and worship God.

With a partner, name some other things that you can do to promote healthy living.

142

Promoting peace is a way to respect life.

God's grace strengthens us to love and respect others. Love and respect lead to peace in our hearts and in our world. Peace comes about when people truly love one another and work together.

The Church community works toward peace by making sure people have the things they need to live. We work so people feel free and safe to talk to one another. We call others to respect the dignity of individuals and societies.

Jesus taught his disciples to value love above all else. He told them, "You have heard that it was said, 'You shall love your neighbor and hate your enemy.' But I say to you, love your enemies, and pray for those who persecute you, that you may be children of your heavenly Father, for he makes his sun rise on the bad and the good, and causes rain to fall on the just and the unjust" (Matthew 5:43–45).

We trust that God will help us to be strong witnesses to his love. If individuals, groups, and nations work for peace and justice, we will have a world of love, not hatred and violence.

WE RESPOND

Design a billboard to show the different ways we can respect life and promote peace: at home and in the neighborhood, in class and on the playground, and in sports and activities.

143

PROJECT

Show What *you* Know

Unscramble the tiles to find the definition for the **Key Word**. Some tiles have been filled in.

TED	M BE	HAS	RSON		A	ND W
~~N DI~~	ORTH	IN G	~~HUMA~~	VALUE		OD'S
IMA	H PE	~~Y IS~~	GE.		CREA	FRO
~~GNIT~~	EAC	ING	THE			

HUMA	N	DI	GNIT	Y	IS		

Fast Facts

Our Lady of Peace is the patron of Hawaii. The Cathedral of Our Lady of Peace in Honolulu is the mother Church of the Diocese of Honolulu. The cathedral was dedicated on August 15, 1843, on the Feast of the Assumption of Mary.

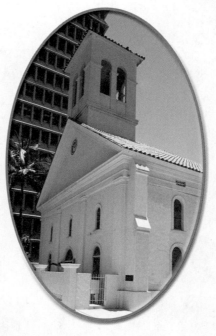

Make *it* Happen

With your class, find out about programs that promote peace in your school, parish, or neighborhood. Decide on a practical way your class can participate in one of these programs. Write it here.

_____

_____

DISCIPLE

Pray
Learn
Celebrate
Share
Choose
Live

More to Explore

Many parishes have Respect Life committees that work to make people more aware of the life issues and the dignity of all people.

Every year on January 22, Catholics are asked to participate in the National Prayer Vigil for Life. Many Catholics go to Washington, D.C. to pray together. They promise again to protect and respect all human life, especially unborn children. Many parish churches also hold prayer vigils on this day.

DISCIPLE CHALLENGE

• Circle the place where many Catholics go to participate in the National Prayer Vigil for Life.

• Underline the sentence that tells what Catholics promise during the National Prayer Vigil for Life.

Reality Check

How do you show you are grateful for the gift of life? Add your own.

❏ eat a balanced, healthy diet

❏ exercise in a responsible way

❏ smoke cigarettes

❏ pray regularly

❏ bully someone

❏ get enough sleep

❏ _____

❏ _____

Take Home

Ask each family member to privately write on a slip of paper, one thing they will do this year to show respect for the gift of life. Have them place their slips in individual sealed envelopes. Tell them to write their names on the envelope to be kept in the prayer corner. At the end of the school year, invite each person to silently reflect on what he or she wrote.

CHAPTER TEST

Choose a word or phrase from the box to complete each sentence.

1. We have the responsibility to respect and _____ life.

2. The value and worth each person has from being created in God's image is _____.

3. All human life should be cared for and protected because it is _____.

4. _____ comes about when people truly love one another and work for justice.

sacred
protect
human dignity
peace

**Write True or False for the following sentences.
Then change the false sentences to make them true.**

5. _____ The Fourth Commandment teaches us to love and respect human life.

_____

6. _____ The deliberate killing of an innocent person is a very serious sin.

_____

7. _____ We can respect the gift of life by not taking care of our bodies.

_____

8. _____ The Church works for peace by making sure people have the things they need to live.

_____

Write sentences to answer the question.

9–10. What are two ways you can show respect for life?

_____

_____

The Sixth Commandment

17

WE GATHER

✝ **Leader:** Good and loving God, you created each one of us in your image and likeness. Thank you for sharing your life and love with us.

Reader: Let us listen to a reading from the Book of Genesis.

"God created man in his image;
   in the divine image he created him;
   male and female he created them.

God blessed them, saying: 'Be fertile and multiply.'

And so it happened. God looked at everything he had made, and he found it very good."
(Genesis 1:27–28, 30–31)

The word of the Lord.

All: Thanks be to God.

🎵 I Am Special

God made me as I am,
   part of creation's plan.

No one else can ever be
   the part of God's plan
      that's me.

☀ How would you describe yourself to a friend or classmate? What makes you who you are?

WE BELIEVE

God creates each person with the ability to show and share love.

Human dignity is a gift from God that makes us all equal. God also creates each person with human sexuality. Human sexuality is the gift of being able to feel, think, choose, love, and act as the person God created us to be. Human sexuality makes us female or male.

Males and females are different but equal. Our differences come from God. They are good and beautiful and are an important part of who we are.

The Sixth Commandment is about love and the ways to show our love. The Sixth Commandment is, "You shall not commit adultery" (Exodus 20:14). This commandment asks us to honor the love a husband and wife have for one another and to honor their promise to be faithful. From this commandment we also learn about the:

• love we have for ourselves

• need to respect and be in control of our bodies

• love we have for family and friends

• proper way to show our feelings.

I show love for my family and friends by

_____

_____

We are all called to chastity.

The Holy Spirit gives us the grace to live as God calls us to live. The more often we choose to follow God's law, the better we live as God's children. We get into a habit of choosing to act in ways that show love for God, ourselves, and others. A **virtue** is a good habit that helps us to act according to God's love for us.

Chastity is the virtue by which we use our human sexuality in a responsible and faithful way. Chastity helps us to respect our whole bodies. It helps us to grow in appreciation and understanding of ourselves and our bodies. Through our Baptism we are called to live by the virtue of chastity.

We look to Jesus as our model of chastity. In his activities, friendships, and family relationships, Jesus showed love for God and others. Jesus asks us to show our friends and family that God is loving.

List an example for each category in column A. Draw a line from each example to all the points in Column B that apply to it.

YOU SHALL NOT COMMIT ADULTERY.

Key Words

virtue (p. 261)

chastity (p. 259)

Column A	Column B
• a television show	• appreciated the differences between male and female as a gift from God.
_____	
• an advertisement	• honored the love between a husband and wife.
_____	• showed that it is important to respect our bodies by the things we do and say.
• a magazine	• encouraged people to think well of and love themselves.
_____	• included people showing their feelings in a proper way.

Friendships are one way we grow in love.

Friendship is a very important part of growing and learning about love and trust. God asks us to be good and faithful friends. Good friendships also prepare us to be the adults God calls us to be.

We learn ways to show our love for others. We learn to express our friendship. We show respect for our family and friends by the ways we listen to them and speak to them. We share our love and care for others by smiles and handshakes and hugs. We say a kind word when someone is hurt. We pat each other on the back after a good game. We kiss our parents good night and hug our relatives when they visit.

God made our bodies to show our love for him and for one another. The Sixth Commandment asks us to express love in all of our relationships in the proper way.

During the next week what will you do to show your family members how much you care about them?

The love between a husband and wife is very special.

The love between a husband and wife is a unique love. A husband and wife are friends, but they are much more. They have committed their whole lives to each other and to the family that they may start. They show their love for each other in a beautiful, physical way that belongs only in marriage. A husband and wife are to share this love only with each other.

In the Sacrament of Matrimony, the husband and wife make a vow, or promise, to each other. They vow to love

and honor each other, to be loyal, and to be trustworthy. They vow to be faithful, or true to each other, for the rest of their lives.

The Sixth Commandment protects the marriage vows against adultery. Adultery is being unfaithful to one's husband or wife.

The grace of the Sacrament of Matrimony strengthens the married couple to live out their Christian marriage. The Church prays that those who are married will remain faithful and true to one another.

WE RESPOND

With a partner design a bumper sticker about the goodness of friendship and love. Then share your bumper sticker with the class.

PROJECT

Show What *you* Know

Write a paragraph about the Sixth Commandment.
Be sure to use the  Key Words.

_____

_____

_____

_____

_____ **Now, pass it on!**

Fast Facts

The gift of human dignity gives us the ability to think, choose, and love. Certain rights and responsibilities come with this gift. We all have the right to the things we need for life. Among these rights is the right to live by and practice one's faith. We also have the responsibility to respect and protect the rights of others. We have the responsibility to act so that the rights of others are being met.

Make *it* Happen

Friendship is a very important part of growing and learning about love and trust. We need to learn to express our friendship. Write some ways you will show love and respect for your family and friends.

_____

_____

_____

_____

↳ **DISCIPLE CHALLENGE** Put your words into action.

Pray
Learn
Celebrate
Share
Choose
Live

Question Corner

Our friendships have an important place in our lives. What would you list as the four top qualities of a good friend?

_____

_____

_____

_____

Look at your list. Does it describe you as a friend?

What's *the* Word?

"Do you not know that your body is a temple of the holy Spirit within you, whom you have from God . . . Therefore glorify God in your body." (1 Corinthians, 6:19, 20)

↳ **DISCIPLE CHALLENGE** What is one way you can glorify God today?

_____

Reality Check

The gift of human dignity gives us the ability to think, choose, and love. With this gift comes certain responsibilities. Check the one you will live out today.

❏ respect the rights of others

❏ protect the rights of others

❏ act so that the rights of others are being honored

Take Home

This week, invite your family to choose a particular time each night to rate what is on TV. Make a chart. List the day, program titles, and your ratings. Rate each program as follows:

Excellent—promotes the Sixth Commandment

Good—some aspects of the Sixth Commandment are promoted

Poor—does not promote the Sixth Commandment

Talk about your results.

CHAPTER TEST

Choose a word or phrase from the box to complete each sentence.

1. In the Sacrament of _____, the bride and groom make a vow to be faithful to each other.

2. Using our human sexuality in a responsible way is called _____.

3. A _____ is a good habit that helps us to act according to God's love for us.

4. Through _____, we express and show our love and affection.

human sexuality
virtue
chastity
Matrimony

Write the letter of the phrase that completes each of the following.

5. _____ The Sixth Commandment

6. _____ Friendship is

7. _____ To be faithful is

8. _____ We look to Jesus

a. as our model of chastity.

b. one way we grow in love.

c. is about the ways to show our love.

d. to be true to each other.

Write a sentence to answer each question.

9. What is one way we can express our friendship respectfully?

_____

_____

10. Why do we look to Jesus as our model of chastity?

_____

_____

The Seventh Commandment

18

WE GATHER

✝ **Leader:** Let us listen to the words of the prophet Isaiah as he teaches the people about justice.

Reader 1: "Do you call this a fast, a day acceptable to the LORD? This, rather, is the fasting that I wish:

Reader 2: releasing those bound unjustly, untying the thongs of the yoke;

Reader 3: Setting free the oppressed, breaking every yoke;

Reader 4: Sharing your bread with the hungry, sheltering the oppressed and the homeless;

Reader 5: Clothing the naked when you see them, and not turning your back on your own." (Isaiah 58:5–7)

🎵 New Heart and New Spirit

Refrain:
New heart and new spirit
    give us, O God,
New heart and new spirit,
    to live in love.

Your word gives us hope
    that there is a way to live
    in your justice and peace each day.
(Refrain)

☀ When do you find it easy to share something? When do you find sharing difficult?

WE BELIEVE

We are called to act with justice.

The Seventh Commandment is, "You shall not steal" (Exodus 20:15). It is about the ways we treat other people and the things that belong to them. It is based on justice. Justice means respecting the rights of others and giving them what is rightfully theirs.

The Seventh Commandment calls us to:

- care for the gifts of creation

- care for the things that belong to us and respect what belongs to others

- not take things that are not ours

- show respect for the goods and property of others

- work to help all people share the gifts of the earth.

The Seventh Commandment challenges us to live with one another in love. We are all part of one human family. We need to be aware of the ways our decisions affect others. What we do to help one another shows our love for God, who created all of us.

Name some ways people your age can live out the Seventh Commandment.

We respect the property of others.

When we follow the Seventh Commandment, we do not take things that belong to others. Stealing is any action that unjustly takes away the property or rights of others.

Sometimes people take things from others because they decide the owners do not need them. Some people may think that taking little things does not matter. Others may think that if they borrow things they do not have to give them back. Sometimes people may pick up things while shopping, and then not pay for these things. In all of these situations people are taking things from others. They are stealing.

However, following the Seventh Commandment is about more than not stealing the belongings of other people. For example, people should not damage a neighbor's property on purpose. Sometimes people cheat on a test, copy homework, or use the ideas of others as their own. These kinds of acts also take something that belongs to another. Often these acts hurt others as much, or more, than taking their possessions.

Jesus lived a life of justice and fairness. He asked his disciples to do the same. He wanted them to use what they had to help others.

From the Gospel of Saint Luke we also learn that Jesus wanted people to repay debts and to live up to their promises.

Jesus praised a man named Zacchaeus after Zacchaeus promised that if he had taken anything from anyone he would "repay it four times over" (Luke 19:8). The Seventh Commandment requires people to give back what they have unjustly taken from others.

Read these situations. Write a way to repay each person for their loss.

Tisha puts her sister's hair brush in her own backpack. She keeps it to use.

_____

_____

Janis cheats at a game of checkers.

_____

_____

Willa gets her father to buy her new sneakers after she loses her old ones on purpose.

_____

_____

Ole hits a baseball into his neighbor's window on purpose. The window breaks.

_____

_____

As Catholics...

John the Baptist prepared people for the coming of Jesus, the Messiah. John the Baptist was a prophet. John preached about justice and how to practice it. He told the crowd, "Whoever has two cloaks should share with the person who has none. And whoever has food should do likewise" (Luke 3:11).

The Church honors John the Baptist on his birthday, June 24. What else do you know about John the Baptist?

HOLY FAMILY CHURCH CLOTHING DRIVE

KEEP OFF THE GRASS

God's creation is meant for all people.

God gave humans everything he created so that we would have the things that we need to live. God asks us to be stewards of his creation. **Stewards of creation** are those who take care of everything that God has given them. The Seventh Commandment teaches us to use in the proper ways all that God has given us.

Together as stewards of God's creation, we must protect our environment. Every day we use some of God's gifts for our food, our shelter, our work, and even for our relaxation.

The words of the Seventh Commandment, "You shall not steal" (Exodus 20:15), are a reminder to use these gifts in a responsible way. People, communities, and nations should not use so much food, water, energy, and other gifts from God that there is not enough for others. The goods of creation are to be shared.

We are challenged to care for the world. It is not only God's gift to us but to the generations of people to come. We must work together for the good of all God's creation.

What will you do this week to be a steward of creation?

Key Word

stewards of creation (p. 261)

We are called to help all people meet their basic needs.

In the Beatitudes Jesus calls us to "hunger and thirst for righteousness" (Matthew 5:6). *Righteousness* is another word for justice. We work for justice when we imitate Jesus. Jesus showed care and love for those who were suffering. He showed mercy to people, especially those who were poor and powerless.

Jesus expects his disciples to share and to be generous toward others, especially the poor. We pray for the poor; we must also respond to their needs.

Saint James made this point very clear in his letter to some of the first disciples of Jesus. He said, "If a brother or sister has nothing to wear and has no food for the day, and one of you says to them, 'Go in peace, keep warm, and eat well,' but you do not give them the necessities of the body, what good is it? So also faith of itself, if it does not have works, is dead" (James 2:15–17).

The Church calls us to work together so that all people are treated justly. We need to stand up for those who do not have the things that are basic to life. By performing the Works of Mercy, we care for the needs of others. The Works of Mercy are ways that we care for the physical and spiritual needs of others. Our acts of love may help people meet their basic needs.

WE RESPOND

Work with a partner to design a T-shirt that shows what you can do to live the Seventh Commandment.

159

PROJECT

Show What *you* Know

Write the letter that matches each term with its definition.

1. _____ justice

2. _____ righteousness

3. _____ Seventh Commandment

4. _____ stealing

5. _____ stewards of creation

6. _____ Works of Mercy

a. any action that unjustly takes away the property or rights of others

b. things that we do to care for the physical and spiritual needs of others

c. another word for justice

d. those who take care of everything that God has given them

e. respecting the rights of others and giving them what is rightfully theirs

f. "You shall not steal."

Picture This

Look at the picture. Circle where the Seventh Commandment is being lived out. Tell what the people are doing.

HOLY FAMILY CHURCH CLOTHING DRIVE

DISCIPLE

Saint Stories

The *Catechism of the Catholic Church* states, "the seventh commandment forbids acts . . . that lead to the *enslavement of human beings*" (CCC 2414). Saint Peter Claver spent his whole life caring for the needs of the slaves of South America during the 17th century. Read more about him at *Lives of the Saints*, www.webelieveweb.com.

More to Explore

Work is important. Through work we help God to care for his creation. All workers should be treated with respect. They have rights, no matter what work they do. Among these are the right to be paid a fair wage and the right to join a union. Seton Hall University, a Catholic college in New Jersey, sponsors the Institute on Work. It helps employers and workers improve workplaces and find a balance between work and family needs.

DISCIPLE CHALLENGE

- Underline the sentence that tells how our work helps God.
- Circle the word that describes how all workers should be treated.

Fast Facts

Green Catholic is an organization that works hand in hand with the Catholic community to promote earth-friendly living. Green Catholic offers information and products to encourage all Catholics to be stewards of God's creation. Visit their Web site at www.green-catholic.com.

Green Catholic™

Take Home

Which of the following can you and your family do to show that you are stewards of creation?

- ❏ use cloth bags at the grocery store
- ❏ turn off electronics when not in use
- ❏ do not waste food
- ❏ take part in community clean-ups
- ❏ unplug chargers when not in use

- ❏ _____

CHAPTER TEST

Write True or False for the following sentences.
Then change the false sentences to make them true.

1. _____ As stewards of God's creation, we are called to care for the world.

   _____

2. _____ The Seventh Commandment teaches us to show respect for our bodies.

   _____

3. _____ Justice requires respecting the rights of others.

   _____

4. _____ Cheating on a test is not against the Seventh Commandment.

   _____

Choose a word or phrase from the box to complete each sentence.

5. _____ requires giving others what is rightfully theirs.

6. Any action that unjustly takes away the property or

   rights of others is _____.

7. God's gifts of _____ are for all people.

8. The _____ requires people to give back what they have unjustly taken.

> stealing
>
> creation
>
> justice
>
> Seventh Commandment

Answer the following.

9. Write one way you can be a steward of God's creation.

   _____

10. Write one way Jesus' disciples work for justice.

   _____

The Eighth Commandment

19

WE GATHER

✝ **Leader:** Let us pray Psalm 119.

Side 1: "Your word, LORD, stands forever;
it is firm as the heavens.

Side 2: Through all generations your truth
endures;
fixed to stand firm like the earth."
(Psalm 119:89, 90)

Side 1: "Your justice is forever right,
your teaching forever true."
(Psalm 119:142)

Side 2: "I call with all my heart, O LORD;
answer me that I may observe
your laws."
(Psalm 119:145)

Side 1: Glory to the Father, and to the
Son, and to the Holy Spirit:

Side 2: As it was in the beginning, is now,
and will be for ever. Amen.

♫ Come, Follow Me

Refrain:
Come, follow me, come, follow me.
I am the way, the truth, and the life.
Come, follow me, come, follow me.
I am the light of the world, follow me.

You call us to serve with a generous
heart;
in building your kingdom each one
has a part.
Each person is special in your
kingdom of love.
Yes, we will follow you, Jesus!

(Refrain)

☀ Imagine that everyone
was truthful. How would
this change the world?

WE BELIEVE
God teaches us what it means to be true.

To witness means to have personal knowledge and to truthfully tell what is known. The Eighth Commandment states "You shall not bear false witness against your neighbor" (Exodus 20:16). To give false witness can harm others and our relationship with God.

The Old Testament is full of stories showing that God was faithful and true.

God promised Abraham that he would become the father of a great nation. Abraham believed God, yet Abraham and his wife, Sarah, grew old and had no children. But God kept his promise and Sarah gave birth to a son, Isaac. Through Isaac, God's people the Israelites began. God's word was true.

Many years later God heard the prayers of his people asking for freedom from

ABRAHAM, SARAH, AND ISAAC

MOSES

their slavery in Egypt. God sent Moses to lead them to freedom and eventually made a covenant with them. God promised to be their God. The Israelites promised to be his people and to live by the Ten Commandments.

Because God was true to his people, they learned to be true to God and one another. By living out the Ten Commandments, the Israelites gave witness to the truth of God's great love for them. The Eighth Commandment reminded them to be true and truthful.

Write one way you will show your family members that you are trustworthy and truthful.

_____

_____

We are called to witness to the truth of our faith.

God the Father sent his Son to help us live in truth. Jesus told us, "For this I was born and for this I came into the world, to testify to the truth. Everyone who belongs to the truth listens to my voice" (John 18:37). We live in the truth when we listen to Jesus and follow the example of his life.

The first disciples knew Jesus. They witnessed his life, Death, and Resurrection. Jesus promised his disciples that the Holy Spirit would come to them: "You will receive power when the holy Spirit comes upon you, and you will be my witnesses" (Acts of the Apostles 1:8).

At Pentecost the disciples received the Holy Spirit and were filled with courage. At once they spoke to the crowds, and the people understood them in their own languages.

The Holy Spirit helped the disciples remain faithful to the truth about the risen Christ.

Faith in Jesus spread throughout the world. However, in some areas Christians faced death if they would not worship false gods. Many Christian women and men died rather than give up their belief in the risen Jesus. They are called **martyrs**.

The word *martyrs* comes from a Greek word that means "witnesses." We may never become martyrs, but we are called to be witnesses to Jesus.

Key Words

martyrs (p. 260)

witnesses (p. 261)

Witnesses are people who speak and act based upon what they know and believe about Jesus.

Like the first disciples, we receive the Gift of the Holy Spirit, too. We receive the Holy Spirit in a special way in the Sacrament of Confirmation. Throughout our lives, the Holy Spirit helps us to be strong and courageous witnesses to our Catholic faith.

With a partner name some situations in which people can be witnesses to the Catholic faith. Then role-play one.

We have a responsibility to tell the truth.

The Eighth Commandment teaches us to

- witness to the truth of Jesus by the things we say and do

- tell the truth

- respect the privacy of others

- honor the good name of others and to avoid anything that would harm their reputation.

To lie is to deliberately make a false statement. People sometimes lie to avoid responsibility or to make themselves look good. However, lies damage our own good name, and they usually hurt other people as well. Lies make us lose respect for ourselves.

If we lie, we need to admit that we have lied. Then we need to tell the truth. We also must try to make up for any harm our lies may have caused.

Another way to respect the truth is to avoid gossip and rumors. When people gossip they often spread untruths about other people. Gossip leads to rumors. A rumor is information that we hear but do not know if it is true. Spreading rumors can hurt a person's reputation.

The Eighth Commandment also addresses the need to handle promises in the correct way. If we promise to keep a secret, we give our word to another person. That person trusts us. If we tell the secret, we have gone back on our word. We have broken the person's trust.

Sometimes people may ask us to keep a secret about something that is harmful or dangerous to them or others. In this situation we must help them. We have the duty to tell someone we trust: a parent, a teacher, a school nurse, or a priest. To get help for people in danger is not "telling on them." It takes courage and is an act of great friendship.

It sometimes takes courage to tell the truth. Name some times when it is easy to tell the truth. Name some times when it is difficult.

We have a responsibility to respect the truth.

From many experiences that you have had in life, you have learned that some people are true to their word. They can be trusted. When they say something, they mean it. These people are honoring the Eighth Commandment because they are being truthful. They are living out the truth in their lives.

Once, when Jesus was teaching about the Eighth Commandment, he explained it very simply. He said, "Let your 'Yes' mean 'Yes,' and your 'No,' mean 'No'" (Matthew 5:37). Jesus expects our words to be true. When we follow Jesus' teachings, we learn what is true and how to live out the truth.

As Catholics...

In talking to others and about others, we must be guided by Jesus' words: "Do to others whatever you would have them do to you" (Matthew 7:12). This teaching of Jesus is often called "The Golden Rule." We should always remember these words of Jesus. They help us to act in a fair and just way towards one another. They also help us to speak about others in a respectful, caring way.

How can you practice the Golden Rule this week?

WE RESPOND

How could you live out the truth in these situations?

- You are supposed to be doing your homework, but you are playing a video game in your room. Your mother asks whether you have finished your homework or not.

  _____

- You borrow something from a friend and lose it.

  _____

- When you buy some candy, the clerk gives you an extra dollar in your change.

  _____

- You promise to go to a party, but something comes up that you would rather do.

  _____

PROJECT

Pray
Learn
Celebrate
Share
Choose
Live

Show What *you* Know

Unscramble the words in the box. Use these words to complete the sentences.

SRTRMAY	WISNSTEES	OISGPS	IEL	RMORU
_____	_____	_____	_____	_____

1. The spread of untruths about other people is _____.

2. To deliberately make a false statement is a _____.

3. People who die rather than give up their belief in the risen Jesus are _____.

4. Information that we hear yet we do not know if it is true is a _____.

5. People who speak and act based upon what they know and believe

about Jesus are _____.

More *to* Explore

The mission statement of the Society of St. Vincent de Paul tells what this group does. "Inspired by Gospel values, the Society of St. Vincent de Paul, a Catholic lay organization, leads women and men to join together to grow spiritually by offering person-to-person service to those who are needy and suffering, in the tradition of its founder, Blessed Frédéric Ozanam, and patron, Saint Vincent de Paul."

↳ **DISCIPLE CHALLENGE**

- Underline the phrase that tells who the Society of St. Vincent de Paul helps.

- Circle the name of the Society's founder.

- Highlight the name of the Society's patron.

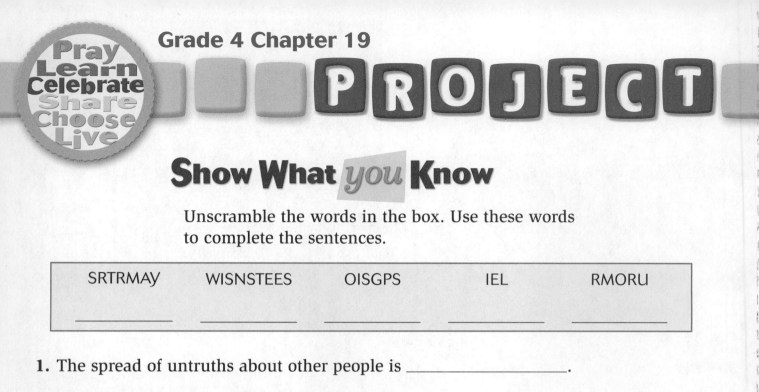

DISCIPLE

Saint Stories

Blessed Frédéric Ozanam was the founder of the Society of St. Vincent de Paul. Frédéric was a husband and father, professor, and servant of the poor. As a young student, he founded the Society of St. Vincent de Paul with others in Paris. Find out what the Society of St. Vincent de Paul does in your parish or diocese.

_____

_____

Question Corner

Survey at least four of your classmates and friends.
Ask: "What issues in living out the Eighth Commandment are of most concern for you today?"

❏ spreading rumors   ❏ cyberbullying

❏ breaking promises   ❏ gossiping

❏ lying

❏ other _____

Be sure to take the survey yourself.
Report your findings to the class.

Pray Today

Jesus, I want to witness to your life today. Help me

_____

_____

_____

Take Home

Look at the survey in *Question Corner*. Conduct the same survey with your family members. Make the time to gather your family together to discuss the findings of the survey. Decide on some ways your family can guard against these abuses.

CHAPTER TEST

Write True or False for the following sentences.
Then change the false sentences to make them true.

1. _____ Old Testament stories teach us that God is faithful and true.

   _____

2. _____ The Eighth Commandment teaches us to tell the truth.

   _____

3. _____ Lies make us lose respect for ourselves.

   _____

4. _____ We respect the truth when we gossip or spread rumors.

   _____

Write the letter of the phrase that defines each of the following.

5. _____ lie

6. _____ martyrs

7. _____ witnesses

8. _____ rumor

a. people who speak and act based upon what they know about Jesus

b. information we hear but do not know to be true

c. deliberately make a false statement

d. people who die rather than give up their belief in Jesus

Write a sentence to answer each question.

9. What can people do to make up for telling a lie?

   _____

10. How can you be a witness to Jesus?

   _____

"For I put water in the desert
and rivers in the wasteland
for my chosen people to drink."

Isaiah 43:20

SEASONAL

CHAPTER 20

This chapter offers preparation for
the season of Lent.

Lent is the season of preparation for Easter.

WE GATHER

✞ *Lord Jesus, help us grow.*

What do plants and animals need to grow? What do you need to grow?

WE BELIEVE

The season of Lent is a time of preparation. Those who will celebrate the Sacraments of Christian Initiation—Baptism, Confirmation, and Eucharist—at Easter are preparing for their reception into the Church. The Church prays for and encourages them. All of us get ready to renew our Baptism at Easter.

This preparing is a way to grow as Jesus' disciples. During Lent we focus on what Jesus did for us by his suffering, Death, and Resurrection. We thank God for his mercy. We think and pray about the new life Christ shares with us in Baptism. We know that we live now by grace, the life of God within us. We can live forever with God because Jesus died and rose to bring us God's life.

Lent, which begins on Ash Wednesday, lasts forty days. The number forty has special meaning for us.

We read in the Old Testament that after God led his people out of slavery in Egypt, they set out for the Promised Land. It took forty years for God's people to get there. These were difficult times in the desert, but God provided for his people.

After Jesus' cousin John baptized him, Jesus went into the desert for forty days. During his forty days in the desert, Jesus prayed and fasted from food. The Holy Spirit was with Jesus as he prepared for his work. During the forty days of Lent, we go "into the desert" with Jesus. Lent is a desert time for the whole Church, the time in which we prepare for the waters of Baptism at Easter.

Lent is a season of simple living. We make a special effort to pray, to do penance, and to do good works. We are called to do these things all year long. However, during Lent they take on special meaning as we prepare to renew our Baptism.

How will you make Lent a time of simple living focused on God and the needs of others?

In groups, come up with ways your family, parish, and class can follow Jesus during Lent.

Pray

During Lent we try to give more time to God, and prayer helps us to do this. Prayer is our conversation with God. In prayer we open our hearts and minds to God. In Lent we may devote extra time to daily prayers and worship. The Church's liturgy reminds us of God's great love and mercy for his people throughout history. It reminds us that in his love God gave us his own Son. It draws us closer to Jesus and unites us with one another. Many parishes gather for the Stations of the Cross (p. 249) and have special celebrations of the Sacrament of Penance and Reconciliation. We pray especially for those who are preparing for the Sacraments of Christian Initiation.

Do Penance

You know that a penance is an important part of the Sacrament of Penance and Reconciliation. Doing penance is a way to show that we are sorry for our sins. Our penance repairs our friendship with God that has been hurt by our sins. It also helps us to refocus on God and on the things that are important in our lives as Christians. Doing penance can help us focus on Christ and his willingness to give so freely of himself. This helps us to act as a true disciple of Christ.

During Lent we may do penance by giving up things we enjoy, like a favorite food or activity. We may go out of our way to practice a Work of Mercy or to give of our time in a special way. Catholics of a certain age do penance by fasting from food or not eating meat on specific days during Lent.

Do Good Works

During Lent we also show special concern for those in need. We follow Jesus' example of providing for the hungry and caring for the sick. We try to help other people get the things they need and make sure that people have use of the goods of creation that are rightfully theirs. Many parishes have food and clothing drives during this time of year. Families may volunteer at soup kitchens, visit those who are sick, and practice other Works of Mercy.

Saint Joseph

In many countries around the world, Catholics have traditions and customs for the Feast of Saint Joseph, husband of the Blessed Virgin Mary. The Feast of Saint Joseph is celebrated on March 19.

We learn from the Gospels that Joseph, the foster father of Jesus, was a carpenter. Joseph trusted God when he learned that Mary was to be the Mother of the Son of God. Joseph provided a home for Mary and the child Jesus, and he loved and cared for them. Joseph shared his Jewish faith with Jesus, and Joseph made sure that the family traveled to Jerusalem each year for the Passover feast. All of this helps us to know that Joseph "was a righteous man" (Matthew 1:19).

Italians and Italian-Americans have a special devotion to Saint Joseph. Their Saint Joseph's Day tradition began centuries ago in Sicily, Italy. There the people were suffering from a drought, and they called on Saint Joseph for help. They asked him to pray to God for rain. The people promised to honor Saint Joseph with a feast if the rains came. The tradition says that rain soaked the area, and the people were true to their word. In a public area they set up large tables piled high with food. All those who were in need were invited to come and eat.

In many places today this tradition continues with a Saint Joseph's altar. The altar is usually made of donated materials and has three stairs as a sign of the Blessed Trinity. On the altar are flowers, food—including specially baked bread—and statues. Food collected is shared with those present and brought to those in need. There are many different Saint Joseph's Day customs, but caring for those who are poor or in need is always an important part of the day.

WE RESPOND

Talk about some special Lenten customs or traditions in your family, parish, and neighborhood. What are some ways you would like to honor Saint Joseph this Lent?

✝ We Respond in Prayer

Leader: The Lord calls us to days of penance and mercy. Blessed be the name of the Lord.

All: Now and for ever.

Leader: Saint Joseph is the patron saint of the universal Church, fathers, carpenters, and social justice. We are called to follow his example of generosity, loyalty, and just actions. Let us listen to a reading from the Gospel of Matthew.

Reader: "Now this is how the birth of Jesus Christ came about. When his mother Mary was betrothed to Joseph, but before they lived together, she was found with child through the holy Spirit. Joseph her husband, since he was a righteous man, yet unwilling to expose her to shame, decided to divorce her quietly. Such was his intention when, behold, the angel of the Lord appeared to him in a dream and said, 'Joseph, son of David, do not be afraid to take Mary your wife into your home. For it is through the holy Spirit that this child has been conceived in her. She will bear a son and you are to name him Jesus, because he will save his people from their sins.' When Joseph awoke, he did as the angel of the Lord had commanded him." (Matthew 1:18–21, 24)

The Gospel of the Lord.

All: Praise to you, Lord Jesus Christ.

Leader: Father,
you entrusted our Savior to the care of Saint Joseph.
By the help of his prayers
may your Church continue to serve its Lord,
 Jesus Christ,
who lives with you and the Holy Spirit,
one God, for ever and ever.

All: Amen.

PROJECT DISCIPLE

Show What *you* Know

In the letter box find and circle these terms about Lent.

```
N O I T A R A P E R P G T R
N O I T A I L I C N O C E R
Q R M O V S M R B O R N C F
S M E R C Y I T D N A O N P
I N O Y R S J W E H Y D A D
X W O T A U O Y T R O F N M
U Q D K T R U O R B Y V E G
X K O Z K N P T G H Q X P E
M D A S H W E D N E S D A Y
```

Ash Wednesday
forty
good works
mercy
penance
prayer
preparation
reconciliation

Write a sentence using some of these terms.

_____

 Ashes are used to bless our foreheads on Ash Wednesday. The ashes are made by burning the palm branches that were blessed on Palm Sunday last year.

Celebrate!

Every third year, the Church focuses on the theme of Baptism for the Sunday Gospel during Lent. Make time to pray for those preparing for Baptism this Lenten season. Write your prayer here.

_____

_____

Take Home

With your family, write one activity for each of these Lenten practices.

Pray _____

Do Penance _____

Do Good Works _____

Put these activities by the dates on your family calendar. Add other activities.

"Through the cross you brought joy to the world."

Good Friday, Veneration of the Cross

SEASONAL

CHAPTER 21

This chapter includes the three days from Holy Thursday evening until Easter Sunday.

The Easter Triduum celebrates the joy of the cross.

WE GATHER

✙ *Jesus, by your Death you bring us new life. Glory to you!*

What are some things you do that last for several days? What joins, unites, or connects the days?

WE BELIEVE

Triduum is a Latin word that means "three days." The Easter Triduum is the greatest celebration of the year. It is during these three great days that we remember Jesus' passing from Death to new life. It is an amazing thing that joy can come from death. But by dying, and then rising, the Son of God changed our lives forever.

We count the days of the Easter Triduum from evening to evening. The Easter Triduum begins on the evening of Holy Thursday and ends on the evening of Easter Sunday. The Church's liturgical year continues the Jewish tradition of counting days from evening to evening. We spend these three days in prayer and worship. Because we celebrate them as the Triduum, we celebrate them as one special liturgy.

Holy Thursday

The Evening Mass of the Lord's Supper begins the Easter Triduum. Many things happen at this celebration. We remember what happened at the Last Supper. At the Last Supper, Jesus gave the gift of himself in the Sacrament of the Eucharist. The Eucharist is a promise that we will share God's life forever.

We remember Jesus' teachings to serve others and the example of service he gave us by washing his disciples' feet. "He took a towel and tied it around his waist. Then he poured water into a basin and began to wash the disciples' feet and dry them with the towel around his waist." (John 13:4–5) We also have a special collection for those who are in need.

As the parish community leaves this celebration, they are not actually dismissed as usual. This reminds us that Holy Thursday and Good Friday are connected in a special way.

Holy Saturday

On Holy Saturday, we spend time thinking and praying. We remember that Jesus died for us and was laid in a tomb. We prepare to celebrate Jesus' new life. We gather with our parish at night for the Easter Vigil. This is the most beautiful and exciting night of the whole year!

On Good Friday, we watched as the cross was carried out of the church. Now, as we wait in darkness at the Easter Vigil, we turn to see something carried into our midst. It is no longer the cross of Christ, but a single bright flame of joy and life. It is the Paschal candle. It is lit at the Easter Vigil as a symbol of Jesus' Resurrection.

"Christ our light," the deacon sings.

"Thanks be to God," we sing in response.

Good Friday

On Good Friday, the Church remembers the Death of Jesus on the cross. The cross is the sign of Christ's suffering and Death. But it is also the great sign of his Easter victory. When Jesus died on the cross, he was not defeated. He rose from Death, and in doing so won over sin and death forever.

In church, the altar is bare, without cloths, candles, or even a cross. We honor the cross with a prayerful procession during the liturgy. We listen to the Scripture readings about what happened to Jesus on the day of his Death. We remember that Jesus was the faithful servant of God who suffered and died so that we might have new life. We also pray for the whole world on this day, since Jesus died and rose for the whole world. And, as with Holy Thursday's liturgy, the Good Friday liturgy does not actually end but extends into Saturday.

At the Vigil, we listen to many readings from the Bible. We remember all the great things God has done for us. We sing Alleluia with joy to celebrate that Jesus rose from the dead. And those preparing to become members of the Church celebrate the Sacraments of Christian Initiation and receive the new life of Christ. We welcome them and once again renew our own Baptism.

Easter Sunday

On this day we proclaim, "The Lord has indeed risen, alleluia. Glory and kingship be his for ever and ever." *(Entrance Antiphon, Easter Sunday)* We gather with our parishes and families to celebrate this most important Sunday of the year. We know that Jesus is with us always.

Make notes about the ways you can celebrate the days of the Triduum.

Holy Thursday	Good Friday	Holy Saturday	Easter Sunday

WE RESPOND

Make up your own prayer of praise and thanksgiving for Jesus our risen Savior. Pray it often.

✝ We Respond in Prayer

Leader: The cross is a sign of both death and life. We were baptized with the Sign of the Cross. It is the special sign of the followers of Christ. On Good Friday we venerate, or honor, the cross because Christ died on a cross out of love for us. His rising from the dead made a sign of death into a sign of life.

Reader: A reading from the Book of Isaiah
"Who would believe what we have heard? . . .
the will of the LORD shall be
accomplished through him." (Isaiah 53:1, 10)

The word of the Lord.

All: Thanks be to God.

Leader: This is the wood of the cross, on which hung the Savior of the world.

All: Come, let us worship.

Leader: We worship you, Lord.
We venerate your cross,
we praise your resurrection.

All: Through the cross you brought joy to the world.

Leader: Holy is God!
Holy and strong!
Holy immortal One,

All: Have mercy on us!

Good Friday, Veneration of the Cross

PROJECT DISCIPLE

Pray Learn Celebrate Share Choose Live

Celebrate! Complete this Triduum chart.

	Holy Thursday	Good Friday	Holy Saturday
What We Remember			

What's the Word?

Pilate said to Jesus, "'Then you are a king?' Jesus answered, 'You say I am a king. For this I was born and for this I came into the world, to testify to the truth. Everyone who belongs to the truth listens to my voice'" (John 18:37).

- Underline the phrase that tells why Jesus came into the world.
- Circle what people do who "belong to the truth."

Reality Check

How will you observe the days of the Triduum?

- ❏ Celebrate the special liturgies at your parish.
- ❏ Remember the Last Supper on Holy Thursday.
- ❏ Remember Jesus' Passion and Death on Good Friday.
- ❏ Choose one hour for a time of silence in your house on Good Friday.
- ❏ Help get ready for Easter on Holy Saturday.
- ❏ Rejoice together and celebrate Easter at the Vigil or on Easter Sunday!

Take Home

Celebrate the three days of the Triduum. Make an e-card or design an electronic message to send to distant family members and friends.

UNIT TEST

Fill in the circle beside the correct answer.

1. Every Christian family is called to be a _____.

    ○ domestic Church   ○ private community   ○ lawful authority

2. When we obey our parents and guardians, we are living by the _____ Commandment.

    ○ Eighth   ○ Sixth   ○ Fourth

3. _____ is the value and worth each person has from being created in God's image.

    ○ Divine mercy   ○ Human dignity   ○ Loving respect

4. _____ are women and men who died rather than give up their belief in Jesus.

    ○ Stewards   ○ Guardians   ○ Martyrs

5. The virtue of _____ helps us to respect ourselves and our bodies.

    ○ hope   ○ chastity   ○ faith

6. Stewards of creation are those who _____ everything that God has given them.

    ○ use up   ○ take care of   ○ do not appreciate

7. The Holy Spirit helps us to be courageous _____ to our Catholic faith.

    ○ parents   ○ witnesses   ○ neighbors

8. The most basic human right is the right to _____.

    ○ life   ○ property   ○ friendship

9. When we obey the just laws of our nation we honor the _____ Commandment.

    ○ Fifth   ○ Fourth   ○ Sixth

10. When we work to help all people share the gift of the world, we honor the _____ Commandment.

    ○ Seventh   ○ Third   ○ Sixth

continued on next page   183

Write True or False for the following sentences.
Then change the false sentences to make them true.

11. _____ Our friendships are not that important in our lives.

_____

12. _____ Each of us has the right to life from the moment of conception to the moment of natural death.

_____

13. _____ When we speak out against violence and injustice, we honor the Sixth Commandment.

_____

14. _____ When we make promises but do not keep them, we fail to honor the Fifth Commandment.

_____

15. _____ Copying homework or using someone else's ideas as our own is stealing.

_____

16. _____ The Fifth Commandment requires people to give back to others the things that were unjustly taken from them.

_____

Write your answers to the questions on a separate sheet of paper.

17–18. Our government leaders are called to respect the dignity of all people. What should we do if our leaders pass laws that are wrong or unjust?

19–20. As stewards of God's creation, what can we do now to make sure that our own children will be able to share in God's gifts in the future?

We Are Called to Holiness

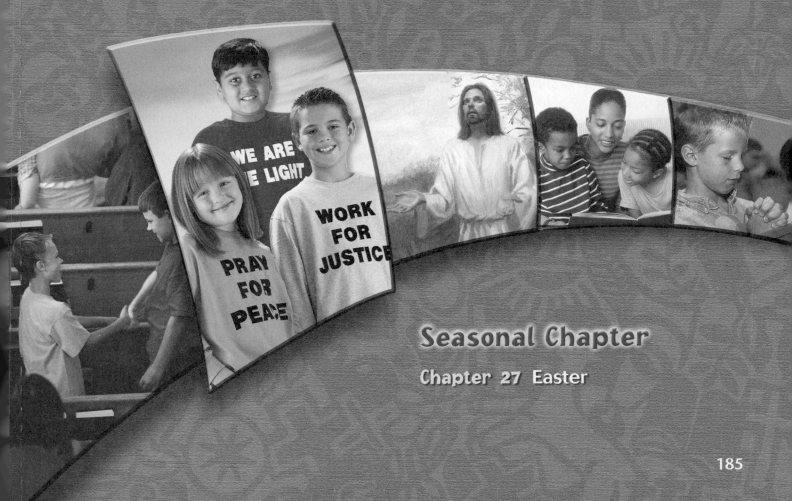

Seasonal Chapter

DEAR FAMILY

Pray Learn Celebrate Share Choose Live

In Unit 4 your child will grow as a disciple of Jesus by:

- recognizing that feelings are a gift from God, and that being pure of heart, and living the virtue of modesty help us to express our feelings as God wants

- trusting God as Jesus did, and having a generous heart toward others

- understanding that the Holy Spirit's gifts and the sacraments will strengthen us

- fulfilling the responsibilities that members of the Church share, and being active in the parish community's work and worship

- living the virtues of faith, hope, and love as Mary did.

Reality Check

"Becoming a disciple of Jesus means accepting the invitation to belong to *God's family*, to live in conformity with His way of life."

(Catechism of the Catholic Church, 2233)

Celebrate!

The Tenth Commandment calls us to have generous hearts. Think about people you know who are generous. Describe what makes them generous. At Mass, thank God for those who have been generous to you.

Fast Facts Your child will learn about blessings and sacramentals in Chapter 24's *Project Disciple*. One blessing that takes place in many parishes throughout the world is the blessing of pets. Christians around the world celebrate the Feast of Saint Francis of Assisi on October 4 by having their pets blessed in the spirit of this patron saint of animals.

Show That You Care

In Chapter 26, your child learns that being a disciple of Jesus means that we are active members of the Church. Look at the suggestions on page 223. Talk about these and other ways your family can be active within your parish community. Choose one way to live out this month.

Take Home

Be ready for this unit's Take Home:

Question Corner Who are holy people you know? Talk about what holiness means. We can grow in holiness in these ways:

- believe in Jesus

- live as Jesus did, working for justice and peace

- pray

- celebrate the sacraments and respond to God's gift of himself.

How can you help each other to grow in holiness?

The Ninth Commandment

22

WE GATHER

✝ **Leader:** Let us ask God to look into our hearts and fill them with his goodness and love.

Reader: A reading from the Book of the Prophet Ezekiel

"I will give you a new heart and place a new spirit within you, taking from your bodies your stony hearts and giving you natural hearts. I will put my spirit within you and make you live by my statutes, careful to observe my decrees. You shall live in the land I gave your fathers; you shall be my people, and I will be your God." (Ezekiel 36:26–28)

The word of the Lord.

All: Thanks be to God.

Leader: Glory to the Father, and to the Son, and to the Holy Spirit:

All: as it was in the beginning, is now, and will be for ever. Amen.

🎵 We Are Yours, O Lord

Refrain:
Help us to remember who and
    what we are:
We are yours, O Lord.

Teach us in your ways for all of our days. Let us hear your unspoken voice. (Refrain)

☀ How is your life different now than when you were in first grade?

187

Feelings are a gift from God.

As we grow older we begin to understand more about the ways we think and feel. Feelings are natural. They are a gift from God. We all have feelings from the youngest age. Love, anger, joy, fear, and sadness are some of the feelings we may have. It is important to understand that people can have different feelings about the same thing. For example, a ride on a roller coaster may make one person happy and another person afraid.

Jesus had feelings, too. Look at these pictures. How do you think Jesus felt in each situation? Why?

As we grow the things that cause us to feel certain ways may change. And the ways we express our feelings change, too. Feelings themselves are not good or evil, but the way we deal with or act on our feelings can be good or evil.

The way we express a feeling either shows love and respect for God and others, or does not show love and respect. We should not express feelings that might lead us to act in unloving or disrespectful ways.

We can call on the Holy Spirit to strengthen us and guide us to make good choices about the ways we act. The gift of conscience, the ability to know the difference between good and evil, helps us to choose actions that show love for God, ourselves, and others. We can also call on people we trust to help us to make good decisions.

God created us to share love.

Part of growing up is becoming more aware of the gift of human sexuality that God has given us. God creates each of us male or female. He gave us this gift of human sexuality so we can show others love and affection.

The Sixth Commandment teaches us the proper ways to show love and affection. It teaches us to respect and be in control of our bodies.

 Name your favorite song.

_____

Why do you like this song?

_____

_____

Does this song respect both women and men? How does it make you feel about yourself?

_____

_____

_____

_____

Key Word

covet (p. 259)

The Ninth Commandment is also about love and affection. The Ninth Commandment is, "You shall not covet your neighbor's wife." To **covet** means to wrongly desire something that is someone else's. When we desire, or want, something unreasonably, our thoughts and feelings can lead us to do things we should not do. Husbands and wives are called to be faithful to one another. They are asked to be loyal to each other.

The Ninth Commandment calls all people to respect the love between a husband and a wife. It helps all of us to know the proper ways to feel and think about loving others.

God calls us to be pure of heart.

By his words and actions, Jesus taught us how to focus our hearts on God. In the Beatitudes Jesus promises us happiness if we love God and trust in God. One of the Beatitudes is: "Blessed are the clean of heart, for they will see God" (Matthew 5:8).

Living by the Ninth Commandment means being clean of heart, or pure of heart. When we are pure of heart, we live as God calls us to live. We love others and believe in God's love for us. Our thoughts and feelings lead us to trust in God's ways and to value our human sexuality.

How can our hearts be made pure? God first gives us a pure heart in Baptism. Throughout our lives we work to make our hearts pure by:

- practicing the virtue of chastity, which helps us to show love for others in an honest and faithful way

- trying to know and follow God's will

- avoiding thoughts and feelings that lead us away from following God's commandments

- praying, celebrating the sacraments, and keeping our hearts focused on God.

In all these ways, God's grace strengthens us to be pure of heart.

RECIPE

On the recipe card, write your own recipe for a pure heart.

_____

_____

_____

_____

The virtue of modesty helps us to be pure of heart.

Being pure of heart requires modesty. **Modesty** is the virtue by which we think, speak, act, and dress in ways that show respect for ourselves and others.

Being modest is an important part of living out the Ninth Commandment. Modesty is about honoring our own dignity and the dignity of others. When we are modest we protect our bodies. Modesty guides how we look at others and behave toward them.

In a group discuss how you think the virtue of modesty could be practiced in each situation.

Barry has just received his grade on a very difficult test. He is very happy because he did very well. His best friend did not do as well.

Yana is going to a birthday party. Her mother lets her pick out a new outfit for the party.

WE RESPOND

How would you explain the Ninth Commandment to someone who has never heard about it?

Ask God for the courage to respect yourself and others always.

Key Word
modesty (p. 260)

As Catholics...

Mary was pure of heart. She lived as God wanted her to live. She was ready to do what God asked. Mary said yes when God asked her to be the Mother of his Son because her heart was open to God's call.

Mary shows us how to speak and act with a pure heart. She was a loving wife to Joseph. She was a loving mother to Jesus.

As Catholics we believe that Mary is our mother, too. Mary wants us to live as devoted children of God.

This week ask Mary to help you.

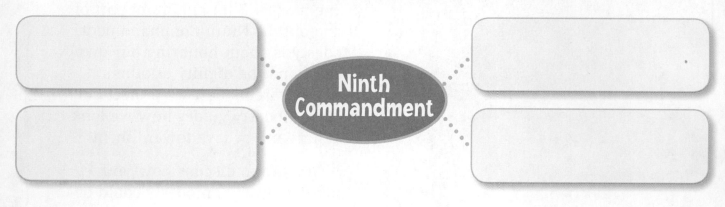

PROJECT

Pray Learn Celebrate Share Choose Live

Show What *you* Know

Complete the word web by writing phrases that explain ways of following the Ninth Commandment.

Ninth Commandment

ON AIR

What Would *you* do?

Imagine that you have been put in charge of a TV network. What would you do to promote living out the Ninth Commandment?

_____

_____

_____

Saint Stories

Born to a wealthy family, Katharine Drexel answered God's call to educate and help children, especially African-American and Native-American children.

↘ **DISCIPLE CHALLENGE** What ways can fourth graders help children throughout the world?

DISCIPLE

More to Explore

Catholic Relief Services (CRS) helps people around the world who are in need. In times of flood, famine, earthquake, or war, CRS is there to help. They help the hungry and those who have to move because of war. This group gives Catholics the chance to work for laws that end poverty around the world. The U.S. Conference of Catholic Bishops sponsors Catholic Relief Services.

↳ DISCIPLE CHALLENGE

- Circle ways that CRS helps people in need.
- Visit Catholic Relief Services at www.crs.org.

Picture This

Sometimes people do good deeds just to show off. Their hearts are not filled with love for God and others. This is what Jesus has to say:

"Hypocrites, well did Isaiah prophesy about you when he said:
'This people honors me with their lips,
but their hearts are far from me'" (Matthew 15:7–8).

Choose a photo from this chapter. Tell the way it shows someone whose heart is filled with love for God and others.

Reality Check

Check one way you will live out the Ninth Commandment.

❏ practice the virtue of chastity

❏ try to know and follow God's will

❏ avoid thoughts that go against God's commandments

❏ pray, celebrate the sacraments, and stay focused on God

❏ other _____

Take Home

With your family, check your local movie listings. Together, investigate the various story lines. Decide if any movie would be a good one to see based on what you have learned about living out the commandments.

Choose a word or phrase from the box to complete each sentence.

1. _____ is a gift from God so that we can show others love and affection.

2. We can be _____ by loving others and believing in God's love for us.

3. _____ are a gift from God and should be respected by ourselves and others.

4. It is important to show _____ for God and the feelings of others.

> feelings
>
> pure of heart
>
> respect
>
> human sexuality

Write the letter of the phrase that defines each of the following.

5. _____ covet

    a. "Blessed are the clean of heart for they will see God." (Matthew 5:8)

6. _____ a beatitude

    b. calls all people to respect the love between a husband and a wife

7. _____ Ninth Commandment

    c. the virtue by which we show respect for ourselves and others

8. _____ modesty

    d. to wrongly desire something that is someone else's

Answer the following.

9–10. Write two ways we can work to make our hearts pure.

_____

_____

The Tenth Commandment

23

WE GATHER

✝ **Leader:** Let us listen to the words of Jesus as he teaches us about important things in life.

Reader: A reading from the holy Gospel according to Luke

All: Glory to you, Lord.

Reader: Jesus said, "Therefore I tell you, do not worry about your life and what you will eat, or about your body and what you will wear. For life is more than food and the body more than clothing. Notice the ravens: they do not sow or reap; they have neither storehouse nor barn, yet God feeds them. How much more important are you than birds!"
(Luke 12:22–24)

The Gospel of the Lord.

All: Praise to you, Lord Jesus Christ!

🎵 **Pescador de Hombres/
Lord, You Have Come**

Lord, you have come to the seashore,
   neither searching for the rich nor the
      wise,
   desiring only that I should follow.

Refrain:
O Lord, with your eyes set upon me,
gently smiling, you have spoken my
      name;
all I longed for I have found by the
      water,
at your side, I will seek other shores.

Tú has venido a la orilla,
no has buscado ni a sabios ni a ricos;
tan sólo quieres que yo te siga.

Refrain:
Señor, me has mirado a los ojos,
sonriendo has dicho mi nombre,
en la arena he dejado mi barca,
junto a ti buscaré otro mar.

Glory to You, Lord

☀ Name some people in your life who are generous.

195

WE BELIEVE

We are called to have generous hearts.

The Tenth Commandment is, "You shall not covet your neighbor's goods." Like the Ninth Commandment, the Tenth Commandment teaches us to look into our hearts and to examine our thoughts and feelings. We try to understand our feelings toward the things that others have.

The Tenth Commandment also relates to the Seventh Commandment. Both of these commandments deal with the property of others. We do not take things that do not belong to us. We also do not wrongly desire those things. When we live out the Tenth Commandment, we do not covet, or wrongly desire, the goods and property of others.

Living out the Tenth Commandment keeps us from spending too much time wishing for the things we do not have. Instead, we should be thankful for what we have. We should work for what we need and work to help others to have what they need.

Are we happy that people have what they need? Are we happy that people have many things that they want? **Envy** is a feeling of sadness when someone else has the things we want for ourselves. Envy can lead to taking what belongs to someone else.

When people rely on God and are grateful for the many gifts he has given them, envy does not become a part of their lives. People who think of others in a loving and giving way develop a generous heart, not an envious one.

Read each situation. Act it out to show how the boys and girls can follow the Tenth Commandment.

- Darryl helped his father all summer. His father gave him a new bike for his hard work. Vinny sees the new bike and thinks, "I want that bike."

- Roberta and Carlos were finalists in the school spelling bee. Carlos misspelled a word that Roberta spelled correctly. Roberta won.

- As an only child, David has been the center of attention for his family. Last March, David's parents adopted a beautiful baby girl. Now David has to share the attention with his new baby sister.

Jesus taught us to trust in God above all things.

"You shall not covet your neighbor's house . . . nor anything else that belongs to him" (Exodus 20:17) reminds us not to get caught up in wanting things. We all need certain things to have a happy and healthy life. God hopes that we have those things. He calls us to help others have the things they need, too. However, when people are greedy they want more and more of something—for example, money or clothing. **Greed** is an excessive desire to have or own things.

Think about these words of Jesus. "Take care to guard against all greed, for though one may be rich, one's life does not consist of possessions" (Luke 12:15).

When people are greedy they want things so much that they can forget the things that are important in life. They forget about the happiness that comes from loving God and others. They forget about living the way that Jesus taught us to live. Jesus taught us that trusting in God is more important than thinking about money and success.

Key Words

envy (p. 259)
greed (p. 260)

envy (p. 259)
greed (p. 260)

As Catholics...

Some women and men become religious sisters, brothers, or priests. As members of religious communities, they make vows, or promises, to God. These vows are chastity, poverty, and obedience. In their religious communities they share everything for the common good. Their way of life gives them great freedom to serve God and their neighbors. They are not distracted by the desire for material things, power, or fame.

With your family find out which religious communities are serving in or near your town or city. Is there any way that you can help in their work?

Describe what is important to you in your life. Why is it important? Does it help you to love God and others?

_____

_____

_____

_____

_____

_____

Depending upon God brings happiness.

Jesus tells us that true happiness comes from loving God and living as Jesus did. Jesus said,

"Blessed are the poor in spirit,
  for theirs is the kingdom of heaven" (Matthew 5:3).

We are **poor in spirit** when we depend on God completely. To be poor in spirit we must be trusting and open to God's will. We need to be content with what we have and find joy in the simple things of life.

People who live by the Tenth Commandment place their trust in God. They follow the example of Jesus. Jesus always placed his trust in his Father. Jesus gave to those who were in need and cared for people who were sick or alone. Jesus asks all of his disciples to do the same. The Church shows that it is poor in spirit when it helps people who are in need.

Saint Paul was one of Jesus' disciples. He tried to help people believe in Jesus and live as Jesus did:

"I have never wanted anyone's silver or gold or clothing. You know well that these very hands have served my needs and my companions. In every way I have shown you that by hard work of that sort we must help the weak, and keep in mind the words of the Lord Jesus who himself said, 'It is more blessed to give than to receive'"
(Acts of the Apostles 20:33–35).

God's Law is LOVE

GOD's Law Makes US HAPPY!

Saint Paul did not waste time wishing that he had the money that some other people had. Instead, he helped those in need. We, too, are called to follow the words of Jesus and live by the Tenth Commandment.

How can both giving and receiving be a sign of trust in others? in God?

Jesus teaches us that God's law is love.

Jesus once said, "Do not think that I have come to abolish the law or the prophets. I have come not to abolish but to fulfill" (Matthew 5:17). Jesus fulfilled the law by living it with complete love for God and others. He showed that following the Ten Commandments brings the happiness that comes from friendship with God. When we follow the commandments, we do so with love for God, ourselves, and others.

Jesus showed God's love. His life was one of holiness, complete love of his Father and service to others. Jesus' life showed that the Holy Spirit was active and working in the world.

Jesus accepted all people and helped them to feel God's love. Jesus called all people to look into their hearts and think of the needs of others. His life and his words showed us that we must love God above all things and our neighbor as ourselves. As Saint Paul wrote, "Love is the fulfillment of the law" (Romans 13:10).

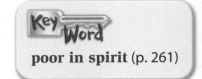

poor in spirit (p. 261)

WE RESPOND

With a partner, make up a song to describe ways that people live out the Ten Commandments.

_____

_____

_____

_____

What will you do this week to be an example to others?

PROJECT

Pray
Learn
Celebrate
Share
Choose
Live

Show What *you* Know

Find the Key Words that answer the clues by writing the letter that comes **BEFORE** or **AFTER** the given letter in the alphabet.

A B C D E F G H I J K L M N O P Q R S T U V W X Y Z

1. Feeling of sadness when someone else has the things we want for ourselves

___ ___ ___ ___
F O W Z

2. An excessive desire to have or own things

___ ___ ___ ___ ___
F Q D D C

3. Those who depend on God completely

___ ___ ___ ___ ___ ___ ___ ___ ___ ___ ___
Q P P S J O R O H Q H S

More *to* Explore

Think of a favorite book, TV show, or movie in which one or more characters are envious and/or greedy. What were the effects of envy and/or greed on the story? Write them here.

_____

_____

Pray Today

Dear God, I want to be truly happy by trusting you and depending on you. I want to be poor in spirit. Help me to

_____

DISCIPLE

Saint Stories

As disciples, we are to treat every part of creation with respect: people, animals, plants, land, water, and air. Saint Isidore and Saint Maria were a married couple who were farmers in Spain. They cared respectfully for animals. They helped the poor. Saint Isidore and Saint Maria are the patron saints of farmers.

↳ DISCIPLE CHALLENGE

- Circle the word that says how we are to treat all of God's creation.

- Saint Isidore and Saint Maria are the patron

  saints of _____.

- Visit *Lives of the Saints* at www.webelieveweb.com.

Reality Check

People who think of others in a loving and giving way develop a generous heart.

Who would you nominate for a "Generous Heart" award? Tell the reasons for your choice.

_____

_____

_____

_____

_____

Generous Heart Award

Take Home

With your family, write out the Ten Commandments (page 77). Then decide as a family one way to live out each commandment in the coming months.

CHAPTER TEST

Write the letter of the phrase that defines each of the following.

1. _____ envy

2. _____ greed

3. _____ poor in spirit

4. _____ Tenth Commandment

a. those who depend on God completely

b. teaches us to examine our thoughts and feelings about the goods of this world

c. a feeling of sadness when someone else has the things we want for ourselves

d. an excessive desire to have or own things

Write True or False for the following sentences.
Then change the false sentences to make them true.

5. _____ True happiness comes from loving God and living as Jesus did.

_____

6. _____ People who are loving and giving develop an envious heart.

_____

7. _____ Trust in God is more important than money and success.

_____

8. _____ The Tenth Commandment relates to the Fourth Commandment because they both deal with the property of others.

_____

Answer the following.

9. Write one way we can be poor in spirit.

_____

10. Write one way that Jesus showed complete love of his Father and served others.

_____

We Grow in Holiness

24

WE GATHER

✟ **Reader:** Come, Holy Spirit, fill the hearts of your faithful.

All: And kindle in them the fire of your love.

Reader: Send forth your Spirit and they shall be created.

All: And you will renew the face of the earth.

🎵 You Call Us to Live

Refrain:
You call us to live close to you.
The signs that you give come from you.
At times when we need help from you,
   you are there with us.

When we come to the water of Life,
   you welcome your people. (Refrain)

When we share the Body of Christ,
   you nourish your people. (Refrain)

When we ask for help in our life,
   you give us your Spirit. (Refrain)

When we hurt from sickness or sin,
   you never forget us. (Refrain)

☀ Whom do you look up to and respect? How is he or she a role model for you?

203

Jesus is our model of holiness.

God is all good and holy. He wants us to be holy, too. So God the Father sent his Son into the world to share his divine life with us. By his life, Death, and Resurrection, Jesus frees us from sin and shares God's life and holiness with us.

Holiness is sharing in God's goodness and responding to God's love by the way we live. Being holy means being like God. Our holiness comes from grace, the gift of God's life that we first receive in Baptism. As members of the Church, we are called to grow in holiness. We grow in holiness when we

- believe in Jesus
- live as Jesus did, working for justice and peace
- pray
- celebrate the sacraments and respond to God's gift of himself.

Jesus Christ is the perfect model, or example, of holiness because he is the Son of God. Jesus put God his Father first in his life. The things Jesus did and the ways he treated others showed how important God was to him. Jesus trusted his Father completely and prayed to him often. Jesus lived by the commandments, loved others, and helped all those in need.

By his words and actions Jesus teaches us to be holy. He teaches us to love God and others, help those in need, and work for justice and peace. If we follow Jesus, he will lead us to holiness. We will grow in God's love.

Name someone you consider holy. Tell why.

We open our hearts and minds in prayer.

Prayer is a way that we communicate with God and God communicates with us. We pray to God by listening and talking to him with our minds and hearts. When we open our minds and hearts to God, we respond to God's invitation to love him. We welcome God into our lives.

Prayer is an important part of our call to holiness. Prayer helps us to be more trusting. It helps us to rely on God and to know what God wants us to do in our lives. God the Holy Spirit helps us to pray and to be open to God's will for us. Praying strengthens us to follow Jesus' example. It helps us to live out our faith.

During his life on earth Jesus prayed often. In his family he learned the prayers of his Jewish faith. Jesus often prayed the psalms, and went to the synagogue to pray.

Jesus' disciples wanted to pray as he did. So Jesus taught them the Lord's Prayer. The Lord's Prayer is also called the Our Father. The Lord's Prayer sums up Jesus' teachings. When we pray the Lord's Prayer, we are reminded that God is a loving Father. We turn to God in trust and hope. We call on God the Father because Jesus his Son did.

The Lord's Prayer is the most perfect prayer, and it is an important part of all of our liturgy. Every time we pray "thy will be done," we are promising to follow God's will in our daily lives just as Jesus did.

Look at the words of the Our Father on page 245. In the space illustrate what this prayer means to you.

The sacraments draw us closer to God.

The Church community gathers together in Jesus' name to pray. The **liturgy** is the official public prayer of the Church. In the liturgy we celebrate the life, Death, Resurrection, and Ascension of Christ. The liturgy includes the celebration of the Mass, the sacraments, and the Liturgy of the Hours.

Christ promised his first disciples: "where two or three are gathered together in my name, there am I in the midst of them" (Matthew 18:20). When we come together in Christ's name, the Holy Spirit is with us, too. The Holy Spirit prepares our hearts to hear and understand how Christ is living and acting among us. The Holy Spirit draws us together and unites us as the Body of Christ.

Christ lives and acts in the Church, especially through the Seven Sacraments. A **sacrament** is a special sign given to us by Jesus through which we share in God's life.

Through each sacrament God shares his life with us, and we grow in holiness. In each sacrament we celebrate God's love for us.

The grace we receive in the sacraments helps us to grow in holiness. As God's goodness and holiness in us grows, we become more like Jesus. We are able to spread the message of God's love and live by the commandments.

When do you gather with your parish for liturgy? What do you enjoy most about celebrating together?

As Catholics...

At different times during the day the People of God gather to pray the Liturgy of the Hours. During these prayers, psalms are sung, Scripture readings are read, and God is praised for his creation and his mercy. Priests and many religious communities pray the Liturgy of the Hours. Some parishes pray Morning and Evening Prayer, which are the two most important prayers of the Liturgy of the Hours.

When is your favorite time to pray?

The Sacraments of Christian Initiation welcome us into the Church, strengthen us to be followers of Jesus, and nourish our faith.

Baptism

Confirmation

Eucharist

The Sacraments of Healing offer us God's forgiveness, peace, and healing touch. They strengthen and encourage us.

Penance

Anointing of the Sick

The Sacraments of Service celebrate particular ways of serving God and the Church. They strengthen those who receive them to be faithful.

Holy Orders

Matrimony

The Holy Spirit shares special gifts with us.

We answer God's call to holiness together, as a community of people who believe in and follow Jesus. God the Holy Spirit helps the whole Church to grow. Together we try to follow Jesus' example and lead lives of holiness. The Holy Spirit helps and supports us.

The Holy Spirit is with us always. The Holy Spirit helps us to listen to our conscience and to make good choices. The seven **gifts of the Holy Spirit** help us to follow God's law and live as Jesus did. We receive these gifts in a special way in the Sacrament of Confirmation.

The **fruits of the Holy Spirit** are the good things people can see in us when we respond to the gifts of the Holy Spirit.

Saint Paul understood that the gifts of the Holy Spirit can change people. He wrote that "the fruit of the Spirit is love, joy, peace, patience, kindness, generosity, faithfulness, gentleness, self-control" (Galatians 5:22–23).

Gifts of the Holy Spirit	This gift helps us to
wisdom	see and follow God's will in our lives
understanding	love and appreciate others
counsel (right judgment)	make good decisions and follow the Ten Commandments
fortitude (courage)	be strong in our faith and witness to Jesus; stand up for what is right
knowledge	know more about God and his love for us
piety (reverence)	show love and respect for God
fear of the Lord (wonder and awe)	see God's presence in our lives and in the world

WE RESPOND

Pray that you will keep an open mind and heart to God the Holy Spirit.

With a group plan a short play that shows the fruits of the Holy Spirit in action.

Planning Sheet

Who:_____

What:_____

When:_____

Where:_____

How:_____

_____

_____

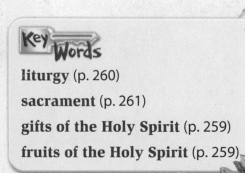

Key Words

liturgy (p. 260)

sacrament (p. 261)

gifts of the Holy Spirit (p. 259)

fruits of the Holy Spirit (p. 259)

PROJECT

Show What *you* Know

Match the numbers with the letters to find the Key Words. Then read each definition.

A	C	E	F	G	H	I	L	M	N	O	P	R	S	T	U	Y
1	2	3	4	5	6	7	8	9	10	11	12	13	14	15	16	17

1. __ __ __ __ __   __ __   __ __ __   __ __ __ __
   5 7 4 15 14   11 4   15 6 3   6 11 8 17

   __ __ __ __ __ __ help us to follow God's law and live as Jesus did.
   14 12 7 13 7 15

2. __ __ __ __ __ __ __ is the official public prayer of the Church.
   8 7 15 16 13 5 17

3. A __ __ __ __ __ __ __ __ __ is a special sign given to us by Jesus.
   14 1 2 13 1 9 3 10 15

4. __ __ __ __ __ __   __ __   __ __ __   __ __ __ __
   4 13 16 7 15 14   11 4   15 6 3   6 11 8 17

   __ __ __ __ __ __ are the good things people can see in us when we
   14 12 7 13 7 15

   respond to the gifts of the Holy Spirit.

Celebrate!

Jesus promised, "For where two or three are gathered together in my name, there am I in the midst of them" (Matthew 18:20).

When do you, your family, friends, or neighbors gather in Jesus' name?

_____

DISCIPLE

Pray
Learn
Celebrate
Share
Choose
Live

Saint Stories

From her earliest years, Teresa de los Andes tried to live every day of her life as a follower of Jesus. She devoted her entire life to God, and at the age of 19 she entered a monastery. Blessed Pope John Paul II canonized her in 1993. She is the first saint from Chile. To learn more about Saint Teresa de los Andes and other saints, visit *Lives of the Saints* at **www.webelieveweb.com**.

↳ **DISCIPLE CHALLENGE** What can fourth graders do today to show that they follow Jesus Christ?

More to Explore

Sacramentals are blessings, actions, and objects that the Church uses to prepare us for the graces of the sacraments. Some objects that are sacramentals are statues, rosaries, medals, candles, and crucifixes. Sacramentals remind us to praise God. They remind us of Jesus and the saints, and they help us to pray.

↳ **DISCIPLE CHALLENGE**

- Underline the phrase that tells how the Church uses sacramentals.
- Name some sacramentals that you have in your home.

_____

Fast Facts

Blessing ourselves with holy water is an example of a sacramental. The holy water and the Sign of the Cross help us to remember Baptism.

Take Home

As a family, visit *Gather In My Name* at **www.webelieveweb.com**. Share the "Question of the Week" for this Sunday's readings.

Now, pass it on!

CHAPTER TEST

Choose a word or phrase from the box to complete each sentence.

1. The _____ help us to follow God's law and live as Jesus did.

2. The _____ are the good things people can see in us when we respond to the gifts of the Holy Spirit.

3. A _____ is a special sign given to us by Jesus through which we share in God's life.

4. The _____ is the official public prayer of the Church.

liturgy

sacrament

gifts of the Holy Spirit

fruits of the Holy Spirit

Write the letter of the phrase that completes each of the following.

5. _____ Jesus teaches us

6. _____ Prayer is a way that

7. _____ Through each sacrament

8. _____ The Holy Spirit helps

a. we communicate with God and God communicates with us.

b. the whole Church to grow.

c. to be holy by his words and actions.

d. God shares his life with us, and we grow in holiness.

Answer the following.

9. Write one way that we grow in holiness.

_____

10. Choose one of the gifts of the Holy Spirit and write what this gift helps us to do.

_____

We Are the Church

25

WE GATHER

✝ **Leader:** Let us sit quietly and think about all of those we know and care for.

Loving Father, thank you for the gifts of friendship, family, and community.

🎵 **Though We Are Many/ Make Us a Sign**

Though we are many, we are one family.
We are one body in your love.

Make us your people, people of Jesus.
Make us your people, called by love.

Blessed be Jesus. Blessed be Jesus.
He came to show us how to love.

Blessed be Jesus, our friend and brother.
He came to show us God is love.

Make us a sign of hope to all in the world.
Make us a sign of hope to all in the world.

Make us a sign of light to all in the world.
Make us a sign of light to all in the world.

Make us a sign of Christ to all in the world.
Make us a sign of Christ to all in the world.

☀ Discuss what it is like to belong to a group, club, or organization. How do others know you are a member?

211

WE BELIEVE
The Church is a worldwide community.

All Catholics in the world share the same beliefs in Jesus and the Church. We celebrate the same Seven Sacraments and follow the commandments. We have different languages and customs, but we are united by our Baptism and our call to love God and others.

A **parish** is a community of believers who worship and work together. Catholics in nearby neighborhoods usually belong to the same parish. Parish members gather for Sunday Mass and the sacraments. They pray, study, and work together for justice and peace. People serve their parishes through different ministries. They have responsibilities in religious education, youth organizations, social outreach programs, and in the liturgy.

A **pastor** is the priest who leads the parish in worship, prayer, and teaching. A deacon serves the parish by preaching, baptizing, and assisting the pastor. All the members of the parish work together to continue Jesus' work.

Each parish is part of a **diocese**, a local area of the Church led by a bishop. The **bishops** are leaders of the Church who continue the work of the Apostles. The bishops are the successors of the Apostles. The authority of the Apostles has been handed down to the bishops of each generation. The bishops continue the work of Jesus that was first given to the Apostles. They act in Jesus' name. The bishops teach, govern, or lead, and sanctify, or make holy.

The **pope** is the bishop of the diocese of Rome in Italy. He continues the leadership of Saint Peter, and the bishops work with the pope as their leader. Together with all the bishops, he leads and guides the whole Church.

List some ways you will show that you are part of the parish community.

_____

_____

_____

We have responsibilities as members of the Church.

Jesus gave Peter and the Apostles help in guiding the Church. At the Last Supper Jesus told the Apostles, "The holy Spirit that the Father will send in my name—he will teach you everything and remind you of all that [I] told you" (John 14:26).

Like the Apostles, the pope and bishops are strengthened and guided by the Holy Spirit. They help us to understand what it means to live as followers of Jesus in today's world.

The Holy Spirit is with all of us, helping us to be Jesus' disciples. The pope and bishops have established some laws to help us know and fulfill our responsibilities as members of the Church. These laws are called the **precepts of the Church**.

The precepts of the Church remind us that growing in holiness and serving the Church are important responsibilities. They help us to see that loving God and others is connected to our life of prayer, worship, and service. The precepts teach us to act as members of the Church. They also make sure that the Church has what it needs to serve its members and to grow.

 Explain to a friend why the precepts of the Church are important.

The Precepts of the Church

1. You shall attend Mass on Sundays and holy days of obligation and rest from servile labor.

2. You shall confess sins at least once a year.

3. You shall receive the Sacrament of the Eucharist at least during the Easter season.

4. You shall observe the days of fasting and abstinence by the Church.

5. You shall help to provide for the needs of the Church.

Key Words

parish (p. 260)

pastor (p. 260)

diocese (p. 259)

bishops (p. 259)

pope (p. 261)

precepts of the Church (p. 261)

We celebrate the sacraments.

Baptism is like a door to the rest of the sacraments. It welcomes us to the Church and to celebrate the other sacraments.

The sacraments change us. As Catholics we worship and celebrate with other members of the Church. Through the sacraments the life of Christ grows in each of us and the Church grows, too. An important part of preparing for the sacraments is learning about our faith. When we read the Bible and learn more about Jesus, we have a better understanding of the Church and our faith. We can discover how to live as Christ calls us to live, building up the community of faith.

The first precept or law of the Church reminds us to participate in the Sacrament of the Eucharist on Sundays and holy days of obligation.

The next two precepts remind us of the need to receive Holy Communion and the Sacrament of Penance. The second precept requires that we celebrate the Sacrament of Penance at least once a year. The third precept requires that we receive the Eucharist at least once during the Easter season. However, we are called to regular and frequent participation in these two sacraments.

Receiving Holy Communion and God's forgiveness in Penance are important ways of nourishing and healing the life of Christ in us. Celebrating the sacraments strengthens the Church and unites its members.

Work with a partner. Name ways you can follow the first three precepts.

214

We have an active role in the Church community.

We are an important part of the Church community. Being a member of the Church gives us certain responsibilities to one another.

The fourth precept of the Church deals with the importance of doing penance. Doing penance helps us to focus on God and what is important in our lives as Christians. Doing penance is also a way to show we are sorry for our sins. That is why it is an important part of the Sacrament of Penance. There are days during the Church year when Catholics do penance by fasting from food or not eating meat. Ash Wednesday, Good Friday, and the Fridays of Lent are some of these days.

The fifth precept of the Church deals with helping the Church help others. As Church members we contribute to the support of the Church in many ways. We offer money, time, and our talents. Just as it takes money to care for our families, money keeps our parish and diocese strong and active. That is one reason that there is a collection at Mass.

Our diocese helps people with housing, food, medical care, education, and many other needs. We also work to share the Good News of Jesus at school, in our neighborhoods, and with all those we meet. This missionary work is our responsibility as members of the Church.

WE RESPOND

The precepts help us to grow in holiness as a community of believers. If you could add one more precept, what would it be and why?

_____

_____

_____

_____

As Catholics...

Each time we gather as a parish for the celebration of the Mass we profess our faith by saying the Nicene Creed or the Apostles' Creed. In the Nicene Creed we state, "I believe in one, holy, catholic and apostolic Church." Our belief in the Church is also a description of it. One, holy, catholic (universal), and apostolic are the four marks of the Church. These marks, or features, identify the Church.

Remember what you believe about the Church as you pray the Creed at Mass this week.

Pray Learn Celebrate Share Choose Live

PROJECT

Show What *you* Know

Read the clues. Then read the four words in the box. Cross out the words that <u>do not</u> answer the clue. You are left with the .

1. Bishop of Rome who leads the whole Catholic Church	priest	bishop	pope	deacon
2. local area of the Church led by a bishop	pastor	parish	liturgy	diocese
3. priest who leads the parish in worship, prayer, and teaching	pastor	parish	liturgy	diocese
4. leaders of the Church who continue the work of the Apostles	bishops	deacons	priests	pastors
5. community of believers who worship and work together	parish	precepts of the Church	pope	deacons
6. laws to help us know and fulfill our responsibilities as members of the Church	Beatitudes	dioceses	precepts of the Church	sacraments

Reality Check

Check the ways you take an active role in the Church community. Add your own.

❏ give to the collection at Mass

❏ share the Good News of Jesus with classmates and neighbors

❏ help with parish/diocesan projects

❏ celebrate the Sacraments of the Eucharist and Penance with the parish

❏ _____

DISCIPLE

Pray
Learn
Celebrate
Share
Choose
Live

Saint Stories

Saint Monica was a married woman who lived in northern Africa in the fourth century. She worried about her son Augustine. His life was going in the wrong direction. Monica prayed for her son. After many years, Augustine realized that only God could make his life meaningful. He was baptized. Augustine was a great teacher of the Catholic faith, and became a priest and a bishop. He was canonized a saint. Saint Augustine's feast day is August 28. Also canonized, Saint Monica is the patroness of married women. Her feast day is August 27.

⤷ DISCIPLE CHALLENGE

- Underline the sentence that tells why Monica was worried about her son.

- Underline the phrase that tells what Augustine realized.

More to Explore

Kidnapped from Africa and sold into slavery, Josephine Bakhita later won her freedom. She began to speak out for Catholic missionaries throughout the world. She was canonized a saint in 2000.

Find out more about orders and organizations that support Catholic missionaries. How can you and your parish support them?

Take Home

With your family, learn more about saints and holy people by visiting *Lives of the Saints* at **www.webelieveweb.com**.

Now, pass it on!

CHAPTER TEST

Write the letter of the phrase that defines each of the following.

1. _____ parish

    a. the priest who leads the parish in worship, prayer, and teaching

2. _____ precepts of the Church

    b. the leaders of the Church who continue the work of the Apostles

3. _____ bishops

    c. the laws to help us know and fulfill our responsibilities as members of the Church

4. _____ pastor

    d. a community of believers who worship and work together

Circle the correct answer.

5. Through the _____ the life of Christ in us grows.

    precepts   sacraments   responsibilities

6. Each _____ is led by a bishop.

    parish   diocese   precept

7. _____ is like a door to the rest of the sacraments.

    Eucharist   Baptism   Penance

8. Catholics around the world share the same _____ in Jesus and the Church.

    beliefs   customs   language

Write a sentence to answer each question.

9. Why does the Church call us to regular and frequent celebration of the Sacraments of the Eucharist and Penance?

_____

10. What is one way you can take an active role in the Church?

_____

We Are Called to Discipleship

26

WE GATHER

✝ **Leader:** The Apostles joined Jesus to share a last supper before he died. While they were getting ready to eat, Jesus got up, took off his outer garment, and prepared to wash their feet. The Apostles were shocked. This made no sense to them. Only slaves washed feet! Peter asked a question that was on everyone's mind:

📖 John 13:6–17

All: "Master, are you going to wash my feet?" (John 13:6)

Reader: Jesus told Peter that he would not understand, but he must let Jesus wash his feet. Then Jesus washed the feet of Peter and all the Apostles before returning to his place at table with them. Jesus asked the Apostles:

All: "Do you realize what I have done for you?" (John 13:12)

Reader: Jesus explained what he had just done. "If I, therefore, the master and teacher, have washed your feet, you ought to wash one another's feet. I have given you a model to follow, so that as I have done for you, you should also do." (John 13:14–15)

All: Jesus, help us understand how to follow your example.

Reader: Jesus gave a powerful example of what he expects from his disciples. If they are to be like him, they must be willing to serve others. At this Last Supper, Jesus had some encouraging words for disciples who follow his example:

All: "If you understand this, blessed are you if you do it." (John 13:17)

☀ What are some good habits that people might have?

WE BELIEVE

The virtues of faith, hope, and love bring us closer to God.

A virtue is a good habit that helps us to act according to God's love for us. Faith, hope, and love are the **theological virtues**. They are called theological virtues because they are gifts from God. They bring us closer to God and help us to want to be with God forever.

The gift of faith enables us to believe in God—the Father, the Son, and the Holy Spirit. Faith helps us to believe all that God has said and done. Faith is a gift that helps us to believe that God is with us and is acting in our lives. However, faith is also a choice we make. Because God created us with free will, we choose to believe. Within the Church community we respond to his gift of faith. Through prayer, the sacraments, and living out the commandments, our faith grows.

As disciples of Christ we must not only have faith and live by it but we must also show others our belief in God. We are all called to witness to our faith.

The gift of hope enables us to trust in Jesus and in God's promise to love us always. We do not rely only on our own strength, but on the Holy Spirit. Hope helps us to respond to the happiness that God has placed in our hearts. Hope helps us to spread God's Kingdom on earth and to look forward to the Kingdom in Heaven.

The gift of love enables us to love God and to love our neighbor. We can love God and one another because God first loves us. God's love for us never ends. He is always there for us.

Key Word

theological virtues (p. 261)

Love is the greatest of all virtues. All the other virtues come from it. Love is the goal of our lives as Christians.

As disciples of Jesus we are called to love and encourage one another. Parents, guardians, families, and teachers show their love for us by providing what we need. We can love and encourage others, too. We can be kind to classmates and to people we meet. When we show love for one another, we are truly disciples of Jesus.

Love is the fulfillment of everything that God calls us to do and to be: "So faith, hope, love remain, these three; but the greatest of these is love" (1 Corinthians 13:13).

 Name a few ways that faith, hope, and love have made a difference in your life.

Mary is our model for virtue and discipleship.

God's plan has been that all people live in his love forever. However, the first humans turned from God. But God promised to be with us always. He loved us so much that he sent his Son to save us.

Mary was part of God's plan. God asked her to become the Mother of his Son. This would mean a big change in Mary's life. Yet Mary's heart was totally open to God's call.

Mary cared for Jesus. She watched him grow and learn. Mary in turn listened to Jesus and learned from him. As Jesus grew older and began to do his Father's will, Mary "kept all these things in her heart" (Luke 2:51). Her faith, hope, and love of God were strong. She stood by Jesus as he died on the cross and was with his followers after the Resurrection.

Pedro Fresquis (1780–1840), *Our Lady of Sorrows*

Mary is the perfect model for how we should live as disciples of her son Jesus. She was Jesus' first disciple.

Like Mary, we can say yes to God in our lives. Mary's life shows us that all things are possible with God. We can call upon Mary to pray for us that we may grow in faith, hope, and love as disciples of her son, Jesus.

What can you do this week to grow as a disciple of Jesus?

_____

_____

The Cardinal Virtues guide us.

Our entire life is a journey back to God who created us and loves us. The Cardinal Virtues guide our minds and actions to lead a good life. There are four **Cardinal Virtues**: prudence, justice, fortitude, and temperance.

Read the chart below. In the third column give one example of how you can use the virtue to guide your actions.

fortitude

temperance

prudence

justice

Virtue	The virtue helps us to	How I can live out this virtue
prudence	make sound judgments and direct our actions toward what is good	
justice	give to God and our neighbors what is rightfully theirs	
fortitude	act bravely in the face of troubles and fears	
temperance	keep our desires under control and balance our use of material goods	

We are called to live a life of love.

Jesus wants us to love others as he loves us. Do you know where we get the strength to love as Jesus loves? It comes to us from God through the community of the Church. Because we have been baptized, we share in the life and love of God. Each time that we celebrate a sacrament, the life of God grows stronger in us. We know that we can count on the Holy Spirit to help us act as loving disciples of Jesus. The Holy Spirit came to us in Baptism and continues to be with us. The Holy Spirit gives us gifts to be more like Christ.

We are each called to be a light to the world. We are called to show our love. "Your light must shine before others, that they may see your good deeds and glorify your heavenly Father." (Matthew 5:16) When we accept God's gifts and share our gifts for the good of others, we are a light in the world. As disciples of Jesus we show others what love can do.

As members of the Church we:

- share the Good News
- pray and work for justice and peace
- visit those who are sick or elderly
- volunteer in shelters for those who are homeless and in soup kitchens.

When we follow Jesus' example and live a life of love, others can see the goodness of God in us. They can see the power of God's love in the world.

WE RESPOND

Role-play some ways your light can shine for all the world.

Key Word

Cardinal Virtues (p. 259)

223

PROJECT

Show What *you* Know

Unscramble the letters to find each word. Use these words to complete the sentences.

PACTNEREME _____   IHFTA _____

TEJISUC _____   PHEO _____

DUCRENPE _____   TERIVU _____

VOLE _____   TERFIDUTO _____

1. A good habit that helps us to act according to God's love for us

   is _____.

2. _____ enables us to trust in Jesus and in God's promise to love us always.

3. To act bravely in the face of troubles and fears is _____.

4. To keep our desires under control and balance our use of material goods

   is _____.

5. To believe in God and to believe and accept all that God has said and done is

   _____.

6. To make sound judgments and direct our actions toward what is good

   is _____.

7. The greatest of all the virtues is _____.

8. To give to God and our neighbors what is rightfully theirs is _____.

Circle the theological virtues. Draw a box around the Cardinal Virtues.

DISCIPLE

Fast Facts

The Pietà is a marble sculpture done by the artist Michelangelo in 1499. When the statue was unveiled, Michelangelo overheard people saying that other artists had done the sculpture. Michelangelo got angry and carved his name down the sash of the Virgin Mary. He regretted this and never signed another one of his works again.

Make *it* Happen

Pope Benedict XVI held World Youth Day 2008 in Sydney, Australia. Its theme was on discipleship:

"You will receive power when the holy Spirit comes upon you, and you will be my witnesses. . . ."
(Acts of the Apostles 1:8)

What is one way you will be a witness for Jesus this summer?

_____

_____

Pray Today

Jesus, you invite me to be your disciple.
You showed me how to love God the Father
with all my heart, with all my soul, and with
    all my mind.
You showed me how to love my neighbors
and the importance of loving myself.

It is not always easy to be a disciple.
I am grateful for the example you have
    given to me.
Jesus, continue to guide me
and strengthen me on my journey
    to be your disciple. Amen.

Take Home

Look at your family's summer schedule. Highlight opportunities to live out your discipleship as a family. Write some here.

_____

_____

_____

_____

CHAPTER TEST

Choose the word *theological* or *Cardinal* to complete each sentence.

1. The _____ virtues are gifts from God and help us want to be with God forever.

2. The _____ Virtues guide our minds and actions to lead a good life.

3. Prudence, justice, fortitude, and temperance are _____ Virtues.

4. Faith, hope, and love are _____ virtues.

Write True or False for the following sentences.
Then change the false sentences to make them true.

5. _____ The gift of hope enables us to trust in Jesus.

_____

6. _____ There are no role models who show us how to live as disciples of Jesus.

_____

7. _____ Mary was Jesus' first disciple.

_____

8. _____ The Holy Spirit is not always with us.

_____

Answer the following.

9. Choose one of the Cardinal Virtues. Write how this virtue helps us.

_____

10. Write two things members of the Church can do to show the love of Christ to others.

_____

Hosanna!

The Lord has risen! Alleluia!

SEASONAL

CHAPTER 27

This chapter celebrates the entire
Easter season.

During the season of Easter, we celebrate the Resurrection of Jesus.

WE GATHER

✝ *Risen Jesus, help us to recognize your presence among us.*

Have you ever gone to the bus or train station, or the airport, to meet a friend or a member of your family whom you have not seen for a long time? What was this meeting like?

WE BELIEVE

The season of Easter is a season of meeting. We meet the risen Jesus in the Eucharist and in one another. Here is a story of the first disciples meeting the risen Jesus.

📖 John 21:1–14

Narrator: Some of the Apostles and disciples were together after Jesus' Resurrection. Simon Peter was among them, and he said,

Simon Peter: "I am going fishing."

All: "We also will come with you."

Narrator: "So they went out and got into the boat, but that night they caught nothing. When it was already dawn, Jesus was standing on the shore; but the disciples did not realize that it was Jesus. Jesus said to them,

Jesus: 'Children, have you caught anything to eat?'

All: 'No.'

Jesus: 'Cast the net over the right side of the boat and you will find something.'"

Narrator: The disciples did as he said, and all of a sudden the net began filling with fish! They were not able to pull it into the boat because of the number of fish! So the disciple whom Jesus loved, the Apostle John, said to Peter,

John: "It is the Lord."

Narrator: When Simon Peter heard this, he wrapped his garment around him and jumped into the water. The other disciples followed in the boat, dragging the net full of fish. "When they climbed out on shore, they saw a charcoal fire with fish on it and bread. Jesus said to them,

Jesus: 'Bring some of the fish you just caught.'

Narrator: So Simon Peter went over and dragged the net ashore full of one hundred fifty-three large fish. Even though there were so many, the net was not torn. Jesus said to them,

Jesus: 'Come, have breakfast.'"

Narrator: The disciples realized that it was the risen Jesus. Jesus "took the bread and gave it to them" and then he gave them some fish, too. This was the third time they had seen Jesus since he was raised from the dead. (John 21:3–5, 6, 7, 9–12, 13)

Imagine you are with the disciples in the boat. What are you feeling when you realize that it is really Jesus? What questions do you want to ask him?

The Easter season is a time of joy and amazement at the risen Jesus among us. It is a time of new life. The Easter season begins on the evening of Easter Sunday and ends fifty days later on Pentecost Sunday, when we celebrate the coming of the Holy Spirit upon the Apostles.

At every Mass during the Easter season, the Paschal candle is lit to remind us of Jesus' living presence with us. We decorate the church building with flowers as a sign of new and joyful life.

Because Jesus rose on a Sunday, we celebrate every Sunday as a "little Easter." The Sundays of the Easter season are especially important. The early Church called the whole Easter season "one great Sunday," one great day of Resurrection.

Easter is a season of joy and happiness because Jesus rose from the dead. We meet the risen Jesus in the people around us. Jesus even told us that when we care for those in need, we care for him.

What are some ways people can meet Jesus in each of us? What can we do at home and in our neighborhoods to share the joy of Jesus' love?

_____

_____

During the Easter season the Church celebrates two very important events in the life of the Church.

Ascension

In the United States some dioceses observe the Ascension on Thursday, the fortieth day after Easter, as a holy day of obligation. Some dioceses observe it on the next Sunday. Whenever we celebrate it, we recall the last event of Jesus' public life, his Ascension. We read about Jesus' return to his Father in Heaven in the Acts of the Apostles.

Acts of the Apostles 1:3–12

Forty days after his Resurrection, the risen Jesus had gathered with his Apostles outside of Jerusalem. He told them that they would receive power when the Holy Spirit came upon them. They would be strengthened to be his witnesses to all the ends of the earth.

> "When he had said this, as they were looking on, he was lifted up, and a cloud took him from their sight."
>
> (Acts of the Apostles 1:9)

Pentecost Sunday

After the Ascension the Apostles returned to Jerusalem and awaited the coming of the Holy Spirit.

Pentecost

We celebrate Pentecost fifty days after Easter. It is the last Sunday and final day of the Easter season. On Pentecost Sunday we celebrate the coming of the Holy Spirit to the first disciples. We remember the ways the Holy Spirit helped the Apostles as they continued Jesus' work. On Pentecost we celebrate the beginning of the Church, and we rejoice because the Holy Spirit fills our hearts, too!

WE RESPOND

In what ways can the Holy Spirit help you to continue Jesus' work?

Call on the Holy Spirit to be with you.

✝ We Respond in Prayer

Leader: Come, Holy Spirit,
  fill the hearts of your faithful.

All: And kindle in them the fire of your love.

Leader: Send forth your Spirit and they
  shall be created.

All: And you will renew the face of the earth.

Reader: A reading from the Acts of the Apostles

"When the time for Pentecost was fulfilled, they
were all in one place together. And suddenly there
came from the sky a noise like a strong driving wind,
and it filled the entire house in which they were.
Then there appeared to them tongues as of fire, which
parted and came to rest on each one of them. And
they were all filled with the holy Spirit and began to
speak in different tongues, as the Spirit enabled them
to proclaim."(Acts of the Apostles 2:1–4)

The word of the Lord.

All: Thanks be to God.

🎵 Send Us Your Spirit

Refrain:
  Send us your Spirit, O Lord,
  And renew the face of the earth!

May your glory last forever.
May you rejoice in all we do! (Refrain)

PROJECT DISCIPLE

Show What you Know

Use each of the letters in "Easter" to write words or phrases about the season.

E
A
S
T
E
R

_____   _____
_____   _____
_____   _____
_____   _____
_____   _____

What's the Word?

The angel said to the women at the tomb,

"Do not be afraid! I know that you are seeking Jesus the crucified. He is not here, for he has been raised just as he said. Come and see the place where he lay. Then go quickly and tell his disciples, 'He has been raised from the dead, and he is going before you to Galilee; there you will see him'" (Matthew 28:5–7).

↳ **DISCIPLE CHALLENGE** Underline the sentences that tell why Jesus was not in the tomb.

Take Home

With your family, plan a special family breakfast. Invite several family members to read the story of the risen Jesus and his disciples on pages 228–229. Share times that family members have experienced the risen Jesus in their own lives.

Pray Today

May the risen Lord breathe on our minds and open our eyes that we may know him in the breaking of bread, and follow him in his risen life. Amen.

Choose a word or phrase from the box to complete each sentence.

1. The _____ Commandment calls us to be happy that other people have what they need and want.

2. The _____ of the Church are laws to help us know and fulfill our responsibilities as members of the Church.

3. _____ is sharing in God's goodness and responding to God's love by the way we live.

4. Christ is always present when we celebrate the _____, the official public prayer of the Church.

5. _____ is the virtue by which we think, speak, act, and dress in ways that show respect for ourselves and others.

6. The _____ Commandment calls us to respect the love between a husband and wife.

7. A _____ is a community of believers who worship and work together.

8. The _____ are special signs given to us by Jesus through which we share in God's life.

9. The _____ sums up Jesus' teachings.

parish

liturgy

Lord's Prayer

Ninth

precepts

sacraments

holiness

modesty

Tenth

continued on next page **233**

Write the letter of the sentence that defines each of the following.

10. _____ prudence

    a. This theological virtue is the source of all other virtues and the goal of our life in Christ.

11. _____ love

    b. This theological virtue helps us to trust in Jesus and in God's promise to love us always.

12. _____ temperance

    c. This theological virtue helps us to believe in God and in all he has said and done.

13. _____ hope

    d. This Cardinal Virtue helps us to give to God and our neighbors what is rightfully theirs.

14. _____ justice

    e. This Cardinal Virtue helps us to act bravely in the face of troubles and fears.

15. _____ faith

    f. This Cardinal Virtue helps us to keep our desires under control.

16. _____ fortitude

    g. This Cardinal Virtue helps us to make sound judgments.

Write your answers to the questions on a separate sheet of paper.

17–18. Mary was pure of heart. She said yes to God because her heart was always open to God's call. How can a fourth grader be pure in heart as Mary was?

19–20. Jesus was poor in spirit. He always placed his trust in his Father, and he asked his disciples to do the same. How can a fourth grader be poor in spirit as Jesus was?

Use the clues to unscramble the letters to make words.
Write the words in the spaces and circles.

1. God's forgiveness through the priest's words and actions BUIONLASOT

◯ __ __ __ __ __ __ __ __ __

2. work of sharing the Good News of Jesus SIMIONS

__ __ __ __ __ __ ◯

3. community of baptized followers of Jesus RHUCCH

◯ __ __ __ __ __

4. attraction to choose sin MAPTOTTEIN

__ ◯ __ __ __ __ __ __ __ __

5. ability to know good from evil, right from wrong EICOCNCSNE

__ __ __ __ __ __ __ __ __ __

6. those who said yes to Jesus' call PLESSCIDI

__ __ __ __ __ __ __ ◯ __

7. person seeking God's forgiveness TENITPEN

__ __◯__ __ __ __ __

8. four books about Jesus' life LESSOPG

__ __ __◯__ __ __

Write the circled letters here.

◯ ◯ ◯ ◯ ◯ ◯ ◯

Unscramble the circled letters to find the word that finishes this sentence:

We can ask for God's forgiveness in the Sacrament of

__ __ __ __ __ __ __.

Now use each of the eight unscrambled words in a sentence.

The first three commandments help us to show love and respect for God. Write a song or prayer to honor and thank God and to tell him how important he is in our lives.

_____

_____

_____

_____

_____

_____

_____

Design a storyboard illustrating the story of God guiding Moses and his people to freedom.

Read each question below. Write the number of the commandment that would help you to answer it as a follower of Jesus.

_____ **1.** Should the students listen to the teacher and try to do their best in all their classes?

_____ **2.** Should someone play rough in a game so that the team can win the city championship?

_____ **3.** Is it OK for someone to keep a CD found under the seat on the school bus?

_____ **4.** Should someone watch an R-rated movie over at a friend's house?

_____ **5.** What can someone do to show respect for family members this week?

_____ **6.** Is it OK to throw rocks at an empty building?

_____ **7.** After someone heard classmates talking about a great idea for the fourth grade play, is it right for the person to suggest it in class?

_____ **8.** When someone hears things that would hurt a neighbor's reputation, should the person tell these things to others?

_____ **9.** When friends are arguing, should another friend take sides?

_____ **10.** How can people respect their bodies as special gifts from God?

Across

1. The official public prayer of the Church is called the ———.

3. The theological virtues are ———, hope, and love.

7. Modesty, patience, and kindness are three of the ——— of the Holy Spirit.

8. To ——— something is to desire it unreasonably.

9. A ——— is a community of believers who worship together.

Down

2. Two of the ——— of the Holy Spirit are wisdom and fortitude.

4. As members of the Church, we are called to grow in ———.

5. The ——— of the Church are laws to help us know and fulfill our responsibilities as Catholics.

6. Prudence, justice, fortitude, and temperance are the Cardinal ———.

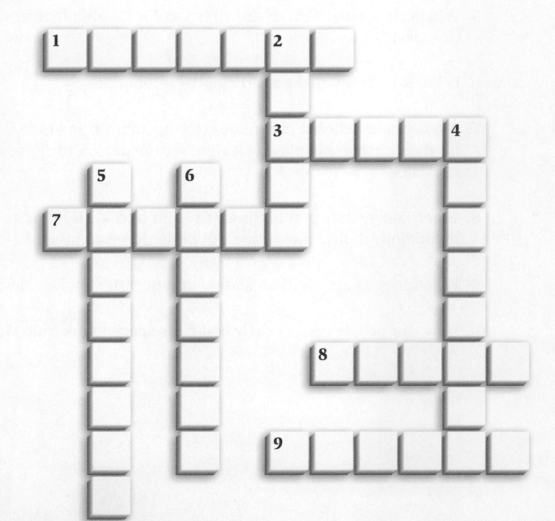

CONGRATULATIONS ON COMPLETING YOUR YEAR AS A GRADE 4 DISCIPLE!

Fold on this line.

PROJECT DISCIPLE LOG

Pray
Learn
Celebrate
Share
Choose
Live

A RECORD OF MY JOURNEY AS A GRADE 4 DISCIPLE

_____
Name

Cut on this line.

My conscience helps me to choose between right and wrong.

A loving choice that I made this year was

_____

_____

Before I make a loving choice, I pray

_____

_____

I will help to form my conscience by

_____

_____

As a disciple of Jesus, I pray in different ways.

A prayer I like to pray

- by myself is _____

  _____

- with my family is _____

  _____

- with my parish is _____

  _____

In Grade 4 I learned about God's Law.

I learned that

- the Ten Commandments

  _____

  _____

  _____

- the Great Commandment

  _____

  _____

2

✂ _____ Cut on this line. _____

As a disciple of Jesus, I share my faith with others.

I share by

○ listening to and reading Bible stories

○ celebrating the sacraments

○ helping people in need

○ praying together

○ learning about the saints

○ _____

This summer I will share my faith by

_____

_____

6

As a disciple of Jesus, I live out my faith by following the commandments.

This summer I will follow the Great Commandment by showing my love for

- God by _____

  _____

- myself by _____

  _____

- others by _____

  _____

7

As Jesus' disciple, I gather with others to celebrate the liturgical year.

The liturgical season I am celebrating now is

_____

This season celebrates _____

_____

I am celebrating

- with family and friends by _____

  _____

- with my parish by _____

  _____

3

✝ We Gather in Prayer

🎵 **Come, Follow Me**

Come, follow me, come, follow me.
I am the way, the truth, and the life.
Come, follow me, come, follow me.
I am the light of the world, follow me.

You call us to serve with a generous heart;
in building your kingdom each one has a part.
Each person is special in your kingdom
     of love.

Yes, we will follow you, Jesus!

Leader: This year we have learned that God's Law
     guides us.

Group 1: Jesus leads us to happiness with God.

Group 2: Jesus teaches us about God's Law.

Group 3: Jesus shows us how to love others.

Group 4: Jesus calls us to live a life of love.

Reader: Jesus said, "I am the light of the world.
     Whoever follows me will not walk in darkness,
     but will have the light of life." (John 8:12)

All: Jesus, we believe that you are the light of the world.
     We believe that you show us the way to happiness
     with God forever. Help us to follow your ways
     this summer.

The Lives of the Saints

Blessed Pope John XXIII

⇾ **Born:** November 25, 1881 ⇾ **Died:** June 3, 1963 ⇾ **Feast Day:** October 11th

What he said

"See everything, overlook a great deal, correct a little."

What the world was like

The world during the lifetime of Pope John XXIII was full of change and war. He lived during World War I and World War II. After World War II, the nations of the world, led by the United States and the Soviet Union, began an "arms race," stockpiling nuclear weapons. This became known as the "Cold War." During this time, Pope John XXIII continually called for peace. When Soviet missiles were found in Cuba, he broadcast a message on Vatican Radio in which he said, "We beg all rulers not to be deaf to the cry of humanity." This message encouraged Nikita Krushchev, the leader of the Soviet Union, to back down. Pope John's last encyclical, Pacem in Terris (Peace on Earth), is considered his "last will and testament" to the world.

Who he was

Angelo Guiseppe Roncalli was born on November 25, 1881, the fourth of fourteen children. Angelo left his small farming community in northern Italy to enter the seminary in 1892. He was ordained a priest in Rome in 1904. Father Roncalli ministered to the working poor and also taught in the local seminary.

In 1925 he was named a bishop, and chose as his motto Oboedientia et Pax (Obedience and Peace). When World War II began, Bishop Roncalli helped Jewish people escape from the Nazis under the protection of "transit visas" from his office. In 1953, he was made Cardinal and Patriarch of Venice.

Cardinal Roncalli was elected Pope on October 28, 1958. Although his pontificate lasted less than five years, "Good Pope John" presented to the world "an authentic image of the Good Shepherd." His most memorable act was calling of the Second Vatican Council, with the goal of renewing the Church. The Council opened on October 11, 1962. Already fighting cancer, he said to a friend: "At least I have launched this big ship—others will have to bring it into port."

Pope John XXIII died on June 3, 1963. His lasting work as Pope—the convening of the Second Vatican Council—is reflected in the date of his feast day, October 11. On that date he launched the "big ship" of Vatican Council II.

What this holy person means to us today

Blessed Pope John XXIII was open-hearted, loving, generous, funny, yet also seriously concerned about the future of the Church. His concern for the future empowered him to act in the present—no matter what. Blessed Pope John XXIII teaches us that we are never too old for right action, and that it is never too late for peace.

The Lives of the Saints

Name _____

Blessed Pope John XXIII

Blessed Pope John XXIII broadcast a message of peace on Vatican Radio to the rulers of the world. He said, "We beg all rulers not to be deaf to the cry of humanity." Imagine that you have the opportunity to broadcast a message of peace to world leaders. Plan a podcast to broadcast your message below.

_____

_____

_____

_____

_____

_____

_____

_____

_____

_____

For saints, games, study guides, and more,
visit **www.webelieveweb.com**.

You are learning and living out ways to be a disciple of Jesus Christ. Look what awaits you in **We Believe** **Grade 5: We Meet Jesus in the Sacraments**.

You will learn about and live out that

- Jesus Christ shares his life with us.
- Confirmation and Eucharist complete our initiation.
- The Sacraments of Healing restore us.
- We love and serve as Jesus did.

Until next year, pay attention each time you go to Mass. Look around you. Listen.

Here is one thing that I know about meeting Jesus in the sacraments.

_____

_____

_____

Here is one thing that I want to learn more about next year.

_____

_____

_____

We are blessed to meet Jesus in the sacraments!

Prayers and Practices

Our Father

Our Father, who art in heaven,
hallowed be thy name;
thy kingdom come;
thy will be done on earth
   as it is in heaven.
Give us this day our daily bread;
and forgive us our trespasses
as we forgive those
   who trespass against us;
and lead us not into temptation,
but deliver us from evil. Amen.

Glory Be to the Father

Glory be to the Father
and to the Son
and to the Holy Spirit,
as it was in the beginning
is now, and ever shall be
world without end. Amen.

Act of Contrition

My God,
I am sorry for my sins with all my heart.
In choosing to do wrong
and failing to do good,
I have sinned against you
whom I should love above all things.
I firmly intend, with your help,
to do penance,
to sin no more,
and to avoid whatever leads me to sin.
Our Savior Jesus Christ
suffered and died for us.
In his name, my God, have mercy.

Hail Mary

Hail Mary, full of grace,
the Lord is with you!
Blessed are you among women,
and blessed is the fruit
   of your womb, Jesus.
Holy Mary, Mother of God,
pray for us sinners,
now and at the hour of our death.
Amen.

Apostles' Creed

I believe in God, the Father almighty,
   Creator of heaven and earth,
and in Jesus Christ, his only Son,
   our Lord,
who was conceived by the Holy Spirit,
born of the Virgin Mary,
suffered under Pontius Pilate,
was crucified, died, and was buried;
he descended into hell;
on the third day he rose again
from the dead;
he ascended into heaven,
and is seated at the right hand
   of God the Father almighty;
from there he will come to judge
   the living and the dead.

I believe in the Holy Spirit,
   the holy catholic Church,
   the communion of saints,
   the forgiveness of sins,
   the resurrection of the body,
   and life everlasting. Amen.

Find other versions of some of these
prayers at www.webelieveweb.com

Morning Offering

O Jesus, I offer you all my prayers,
works, and sufferings of this day
for all intentions of your most
Sacred Heart. Amen.

Evening Prayer

Dear God, before I sleep
I want to thank you for this day
so full of your kindness and your joy.
I close my eyes to rest
safe in your loving care.

Grace Before Meals

Bless † us, O Lord,
    and these your gifts,
which we are about to receive
    from your goodness.
Through Christ our Lord. Amen.

Grace After Meals

We give you thanks, almighty God,
for these and all your gifts
which we have received through
Christ our Lord. Amen.

Act of Faith

O God, we believe in all that Jesus has taught
us about you. We place all our trust in you
because of your great love for us.

Holy, Holy, Holy

Holy, Holy, Holy Lord God of hosts.
Heaven and earth are full of your glory.
Hosanna in the highest.
Blessed is he who comes in
the name of the Lord.
Hosanna in the highest.

Prayer to the Holy Spirit

Come, Holy Spirit, fill the hearts of your faithful.
And kindle in them the fire of your love.

Send forth your Spirit and they
    shall be created.
And you will renew the face of the earth.

Act of Hope

O God, we never give up on your love.
We have hope and will work for your kingdom
to come and for a life that lasts forever with
you in heaven.

Act of Love

O God, we love you above all things.
Help us to love ourselves and one another
as Jesus taught us to do.

Prayer Before the Blessed Sacrament

Jesus,
you are God-with-us,
especially in this sacrament
of the Eucharist.
You love me as I am
and help me grow.

Come and be with me
in all my joys and sorrows.
Help me share your peace and love
with everyone I meet.
I ask in your name.
Amen.

Prayer for Vocations

Dear God,
you have a great and loving plan
for our world and for me.
I wish to share in that plan fully,
faithfully, and joyfully.
Help me to understand what it is
you wish me to do with my life.

- Will I be called to the priesthood
  or religious life?
- Will I be called to live a married life?
- Will I be called to live a single life?

Help me to be attentive to the signs
that you give me about preparing
for the future.

And once I have heard and understood your
call, give me the strength and the grace to
follow it with generosity and love. Amen.

Hail, Holy Queen

Hail, holy Queen, mother of mercy,
hail, our life, our sweetness, and our hope.
To you we cry, the children of Eve;
to you we send up our sighs,
mourning and weeping in this land of exile.
Turn, then, most gracious advocate,
your eyes of mercy toward us;
lead us home at last
and show us the blessed fruit of your womb,
   Jesus:
O clement, O loving, O sweet Virgin Mary.

Prayer for Peace

Lord, make me an instrument of your peace:
where there is hatred, let me sow love;
where there is injury, pardon;
where there is doubt, faith;
where there is despair, hope;
where there is darkness, light;
where there is sadness, joy.

O divine Master, grant that I may not so
   much seek
to be consoled as to console,
to be understood as to understand,
to be loved as to love.
For it is in giving that we receive,
it is in pardoning that we are pardoned,
it is in dying that we are born to eternal life.
Amen.

Saint Francis of Assisi

The Rosary

A rosary is made up of groups of beads arranged in a circle. It begins with a cross followed by one large bead and three small ones. The next large bead (just before the medal) begins the first "decade." Each decade consists of one large bead followed by ten smaller beads.

Begin to pray the Rosary with the Sign of the Cross. Recite the Apostles' Creed. Then pray one Our Father, three Hail Marys, and one Glory Be to the Father.

To pray each decade, say an Our Father on the large bead and a Hail Mary on each of the ten smaller beads. Close each decade by praying the Glory Be to the Father. Pray the Hail, Holy Queen as the last prayer of the Rosary.

The mysteries of the Rosary are special events in the lives of Jesus and Mary. As you pray each decade, think of the appropriate Joyful Mystery, Sorrowful Mystery, Glorious Mystery, or Mystery of Light.

The Five Joyful Mysteries

1. The Annunciation
2. The Visitation
3. The Birth of Jesus
4. The Presentation of Jesus in the Temple
5. The Finding of Jesus in the Temple

The Five Sorrowful Mysteries

1. The Agony in the Garden
2. The Scourging at the Pillar
3. The Crowning with Thorns
4. The Carrying of the Cross
5. The Crucifixion and Death of Jesus

The Five Glorious Mysteries

1. The Resurrection
2. The Ascension
3. The Descent of the Holy Spirit upon the Apostles
4. The Assumption of Mary into Heaven
5. The Coronation of Mary as Queen of Heaven

The Five Mysteries of Light

1. Jesus' Baptism in the Jordan
2. The Miracle at the Wedding at Cana
3. Jesus Announces the Kingdom of God
4. The Transfiguration
5. The Institution of the Eucharist

Stations of the Cross

From the earliest days of the Church, Christians remembered Jesus' life and Death by visiting and praying at the places where Jesus lived, suffered, died, and rose from the dead.

As the Church spread to other countries, not everyone could travel to the Holy Land. So local churches began inviting people to "follow in the footsteps of Jesus" without leaving home. "Stations," or places to stop and pray, were made so that stay-at-home pilgrims could "walk the way of the cross" in their own parish churches. We do the same today, especially during Lent.

There are fourteen "stations," or stops. At each one, we pause and think about what is happening at the station.

1. Jesus is condemned to die.
2. Jesus takes up his cross.
3. Jesus falls the first time.
4. Jesus meets his mother.
5. Simon helps Jesus carry his cross.
6. Veronica wipes the face of Jesus.
7. Jesus falls the second time.
8. Jesus meets the women of Jerusalem.
9. Jesus falls the third time.
10. Jesus is stripped of his garments.
11. Jesus is nailed to the cross.
12. Jesus dies on the cross.
13. Jesus is taken down from the cross.
14. Jesus is laid in the tomb.

The Seven Sacraments

The Sacraments of Christian Initiation

Baptism

Confirmation

Eucharist

The Sacraments of Healing

Penance and Reconciliation

Anointing of the Sick

The Sacraments at the Service of Communion

Holy Orders

Matrimony

Note:

The parts of the Mass are found on pages 108–111.

The parts of the Sacrament of Penance and Reconciliation are found on pages 52 to 54.

The Beatitudes are found on pages 28 and 29.

The Corporal and Spiritual Works of Mercy are found on pages 102 and 103.

An examination of conscience is found in *Living God's Laws,* pages 251 through 254.

LIVING GOD'S LAWS

When we examine our conscience we can thank God for giving us the strength to make good choices. Reflecting on the choices we have made helps us to make choices that bring us closer to God.

Take a few moments to think quietly and prayerfully about ways you follow each of the commandments.

Fold on this line.

Ninth Commandment:

You shall not covet your neighbor's wife.

Do I always act on my feelings? Should I?

Do I try not to give in to temptation?

Do I pray for strength and guidance in making good choices?

Have I been responsible about the things I want?

Do I stay away from things and people who do not value human sexuality?

Do I try to show my feelings in a respectful way?

Do I try to do the things God wants me to do?

In what ways do I practice the virtue of modesty?

Tenth Commandment:

You shall not covet your neighbor's goods.

Do I wish that I had things that belong to others?

Am I sad when others have things that I would like?

Do I trust in God?

Am I willing to share with others?

When I get money as a gift or for my allowance, do I give some of it to the poor and needy in my community?

Am I happy with what I have or am I always asking for more things?

First Commandment:

I am the LORD your God: You shall not have strange gods before me.

Do I try to love God above all things?

Do I really believe in, trust, and love God?

Do I pray to God sometime each day?

How do I encourage others to trust in God?

How do I take an active part in the worship of God, especially in the Mass and the other sacraments?

How do I try to learn more about the Catholic faith?

Fold on this line.

Eighth Commandment:

You shall not bear false witness against your neighbor.

Have I spoken and acted upon my belief in Jesus?

Have I trusted in God's Word?

Have I been true to the teachings of the Catholic faith at home and in school?

Have I taken responsibility for my words and been truthful?

Have I respected the privacy of others?

Have I done the things I said I would do?

Have I made promises that I did not keep?

Have I thanked those who are trustworthy and faithful?

Second Commandment:

You shall not take the name of the LORD your God in vain.

Do I respect God's name and the name of Jesus?

How have I used God's name?

Have I called on God and asked him to be with me?

How do I use the names of Mary and all the saints?

Have I respected the names of my family members, friends, and teachers?

Do I have respect for all the places where God is worshiped?

How do I act when I am in church?

Third Commandment:

Remember to keep holy the LORD's Day.

How have I kept the Lord's Day holy?

What do I do to participate in Mass every Sunday?

On Sundays in what ways have I:

rested and relaxed?

shared time with my family?

helped others?

remembered God?

praised and thanked God?

Fold on this line.

Seventh Commandment:

You shall not steal.

Have I cared for the gifts of creation?

Have I taken care of my belongings?

Have I taken things that do not belong to me?

Have I respected the property of others?

Have I been honest in taking tests and playing games?

Have I shared what I have with those who are in need?

Have I worked with my family, parish, or school to care for those who are poor or to make their lives better?

Have I performed Works of Mercy?

Fourth Commandment:
Honor your father and your mother.

Do I obey my parents in all that they ask of me?

Have I thanked my parents or guardians for all that they do?

Do I respect my brothers and sisters?

Do I help them?

Do I settle disagreements without fighting or arguing?

Do I obey my grandparents and respect them?

How have I showed respect for older people?

Do I obey my teachers and others in authority?

Do I obey police officers, crossing guards, firefighters, and other officials?

Have I followed the laws of my city, state, and country?

Fold on this line.

Fifth Commandment:
You shall not kill.

Have I respected the dignity of all people?

Have I shown by my actions that all people have the right to life?

Have I lived each day in a healthy way?

Have I done anything that could harm myself or others?

Have I spoken out against violence and injustice?

Have I lived in peace with my family and neighbors?

Sixth Commandment:
You shall not commit adultery.

Do I appreciate the differences among my classmates and family members?

Do I honor myself as special and created by God?

Do my actions show love and respect for myself and others?

Do I use my body in responsible and faithful ways?

In what ways do I express my affection for my friends and family?

Do I value my friendships?

Living the Beatitudes

Blessed are they...

Saint Thérèse of the Child Jesus

Being poor in spirit means depending on God for everything. Even as a little girl, Thérèse knew that everything she had came from God. She loved God as much as she could. She thought of herself as a little flower in God's garden.

When she was only fifteen, she entered a monastery of religious sisters. There she prayed for the whole world. Before she died, she promised to spend her Heaven in doing good upon earth. Her feast day is October 1.

"Blessed are the poor in spirit, for theirs is the kingdom of heaven."

(Matthew 5:3)

Fold on this line.

Blessed are they...

The Martyrs of Uganda

The martyrs of Uganda were a group of twenty-two young men, led by Charles Lwanga. They served in the household of a tribal chief who became angry when these young men insisted on living and worshiping as Christians. They were killed because of this. The feast day of Saint Charles Lwanga and his companions, the martyrs of Uganda, is June 3.

"Blessed are they who are persecuted for the sake of righteousness, for theirs is the kingdom of heaven."

(Matthew 5:10)

Blessed are they...

Saint Edith Stein

Edith Stein was born in Germany in 1891. She loved to read and to learn. She became a teacher of philosophy, which includes the study of wisdom. After reading the life of Saint Teresa of Avila, Edith Stein discovered the wisdom of Christ. She, who had been born Jewish, became a Catholic and entered a Carmelite monastery.

At that time in Germany, Jews were being persecuted. Edith's community tried to keep her safe by moving her to Holland. Yet, in Holland she was taken to a prison camp. Before she was killed there, she suffered with and tried to comfort the people with her, especially the children. She died in 1942 and was declared a saint in 1998. Her feast day is August 9.

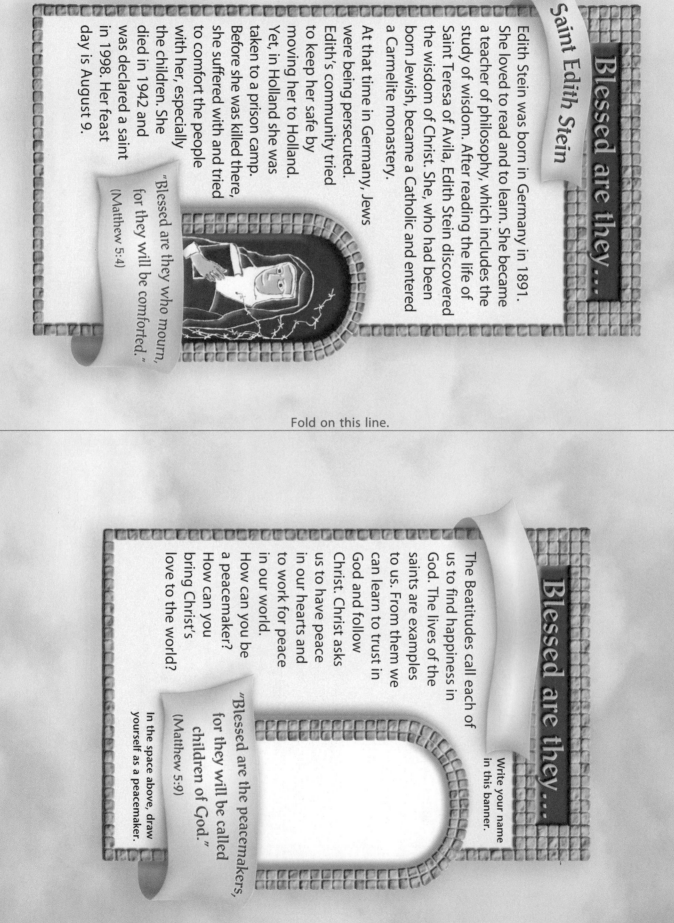

"Blessed are they who mourn, for they will be comforted."
(Matthew 5:4)

Fold on this line.

Blessed are they...

Write your name in this banner.

The Beatitudes call each of us to find happiness in God. The lives of the saints are examples to us. From them we can learn to trust in God and follow Christ. Christ asks us to have peace in our hearts and to work for peace in our world.

How can you be a peacemaker? How can you bring Christ's love to the world?

"Blessed are the peacemakers, for they will be called children of God."
(Matthew 5:9)

In the space above, draw yourself as a peacemaker.

Blessed are they...

Saint Rose Philippine Duchesne

Rose Philippine Duchesne was a missionary to the United States. She was born in France, and was sent to Missouri. In St. Charles, she founded the first convent of the Society of the Sacred Heart in the United States. She had a special love for native Americans, and worked among the Potawatomi tribe in Kansas.

Saint Rose always felt that she was a failure as a missionary because she could never learn the Potawatomi language. However, she was successful. She was patient and respectful to the Potawatomi people. Her heart was always with God, and she spent much time in prayer. The tribe could sense her prayers for them, and they called her "Woman Who Prays Always." Her feast day is November 18.

"Blessed are the meek, for they will inherit the land." (Matthew 5:5)

Fold on this line.

Blessed are they...

Saint Paul

Saint Paul's original name was Saul, and he persecuted the followers of Christ. Jesus himself appeared to Saul and asked, "Why are you persecuting me?" (Acts of the Apostles 9:4). Then Saul realized that when he persecuted Christians he was persecuting Christ himself.

The enemy of Christians, Saul, became the great Apostle of Jesus, Paul. He traveled from city to city, country to country, to tell the Good News of Jesus Christ. He wrote to the early followers of Jesus, "Everything belongs to you . . . and you to Christ" (1 Corinthians 3:21–23). The Feast of the Conversion of Saint Paul is January 25.

"Blessed are the clean of heart, for they will see God." (Matthew 5:8)

Blessed are they...

Saint Vincent de Paul and Saint Louise de Marillac

To "hunger and thirst" for something means to want something very badly. Vincent de Paul knew what it was to want justice since he had once been forced into slavery by pirates. When he escaped, he began to care for those who were poor and in need. He asked Louise de Marillac to help him, and together they founded the Daughters of Charity. The sisters of this community still serve the poor today. The sisters work in schools and hospitals, in services to children and the elderly, and in parishes. Saint Louise is the patroness of social workers.

Vincent also founded the Congregation of the Mission. This is a community of priests and brothers who preach, give retreats, work in parishes, and teach in schools. Saint Vincent's feast day is September 27. Saint Louise's feast day is March 15.

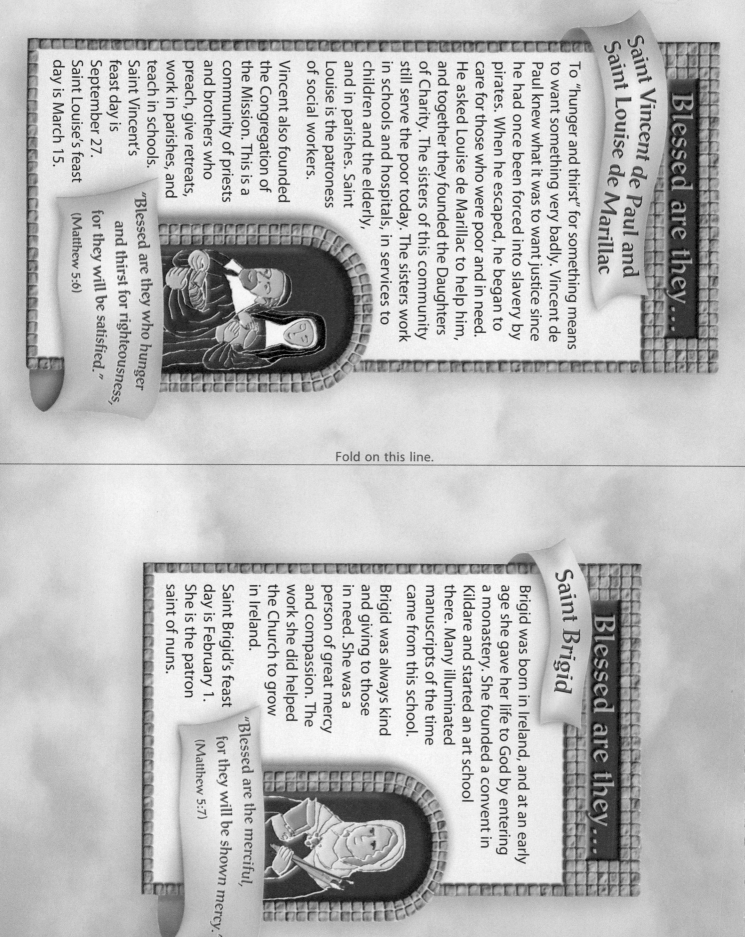

"Blessed are they who hunger and thirst for righteousness, for they will be satisfied."
(Matthew 5:6)

Fold on this line.

Blessed are they...

Saint Brigid

Brigid was born in Ireland, and at an early age she gave her life to God by entering a monastery. She founded a convent in Kildare and started an art school there. Many illuminated manuscripts of the time came from this school.

Brigid was always kind and giving to those in need. She was a person of great mercy and compassion. The work she did helped the Church to grow in Ireland.

Saint Brigid's feast day is February 1. She is the patron saint of nuns.

"Blessed are the merciful, for they will be shown mercy."
(Matthew 5:7)

Glossary

absolution (p. 53)
God's forgiveness of sins through the words and actions of the priest

assembly (p. 108)
the community of people gathered to worship in the name of Jesus Christ

Beatitudes (p. 28)
teachings of Jesus that describe the way to live as his disciples

bishops (p. 212)
leaders of the Church who continue the work of the Apostles

bless (p. 94)
to dedicate someone or something to God or to make holy in God's name

Blessed Trinity (p. 21)
the Three Persons in One God: God the Father, God the Son, and God the Holy Spirit

Cardinal Virtues (p. 222)
prudence, justice, fortitude, and temperance

chastity (p. 149)
the virtue by which we use our human sexuality in a responsible and faithful way

Church (p. 22)
the community of people who are baptized and follow Jesus Christ

conscience (p. 45)
the ability to know the difference between good and evil, right and wrong

Consecration (p. 110)
the part of the Eucharistic Prayer when, by the power of the Holy Spirit and through the words and actions of the priest, the bread and wine become the Body and Blood of Christ

Corporal Works of Mercy (p. 102)
things that we do to care for the physical needs of others

covenant (p. 76)
a special agreement between God and his people

covet (p. 189)
to wrongly desire something that is someone else's

diocese (p. 212)
a local area of the Church led by a bishop

disciples (p. 20)
those who said yes to Jesus' call to follow him

domestic Church (p. 133)
the Church in the home, which every Christian family is called to be

envy (p. 196)
a feeling of sadness when someone else has the things we want for ourselves

Eucharistic Prayer (p. 110)
the Church's greatest prayer of praise and thanksgiving to God

examination of conscience (p. 47)
the act of determining whether the choices we have made showed love for God, ourselves, and others

free will (p. 36)
the freedom to decide when and how to act

fruits of the Holy Spirit (p. 207)
the good things people can see in us when we respond to the gifts of the Holy Spirit

gifts of the Holy Spirit (p. 207)
the seven gifts which help us to follow God's law and live as Jesus did

grace (p. 22)
the gift of God's life in us

greed (p. 197)
an excessive desire to have or own things

holy day of obligation (p. 101)
a day that is set apart to celebrate a special event in the life of Jesus, Mary, or the saints

homily (p. 109)
a talk given by the priest or deacon that helps us to understand the readings and to grow as faithful followers of Jesus

human dignity (p. 140)
the value and worth each person has from being created in God's image

human rights (p. 79)
the basic rights that all people have

idolatry (p. 86)
giving worship to a creature or thing instead of God

Incarnation (p. 20)
the truth that the Son of God became man

justice (p. 30)
respecting the rights of others and giving them what is rightfully theirs

Kingdom of God (p. 30)
the power of God's love active in the world

liturgy (p. 206)
the official public prayer of the Church

Liturgy of the Eucharist (p. 110)
the part of the Mass in which the Death and Resurrection of Christ are made present again; our gifts of bread and wine become the Body and Blood of Christ, which we receive in Holy Communion

Liturgy of the Word (p. 108)
the part of the Mass when we listen and respond to God's Word

martyrs (p. 165)
people who die rather than give up their belief in the risen Jesus

Mass (p. 108)
the celebration of the Eucharist

mission (p. 31)
the work of sharing the Good News of Jesus Christ and spreading the Kingdom of God

modesty (p. 191)
the virtue by which we think, speak, act, and dress in ways that show respect for ourselves and others

mortal sin (p. 36)
very serious sin that breaks a person's friendship with God

Original Sin (p. 22)
the first sin committed by the first human beings

parish (p. 212)
a community of believers who worship and work together

pastor (p. 212)
the priest who leads the parish in worship, prayer, and teaching

peace (p. 28)
the freedom that comes from loving and trusting God and respecting all people

penitent (p. 53)
the person seeking God's forgiveness in the Sacrament of Penance

poor in spirit (p. 198)
those who depend on God completely

pope (p. 212)
the Bishop of Rome, who leads the whole Catholic Church

prayer (p. 85)
listening and talking to God with our minds and hearts

precepts of the Church (p. 213)
laws to help us know and fulfill our responsibilities as members of the Church

psalm (p. 92)
a song of praise to honor the Lord

reverence (p. 93)
honor, love, and respect

Sabbath (p. 100)
the day of rest set apart to honor God in a special way

sacrament (p. 206)
a special sign given to us by Jesus through which we share in God's life

sacred (p. 94)
another word for holy

Savior (p. 22)
a title given to Jesus because he died and rose to save us from sin

sin (p. 36)
a thought, word, or action against God's law

Spiritual Works of Mercy (p. 103)
things that we do to care for the minds, hearts, and souls of others

stewards of creation (p. 158)
those who take care of everything God has given them

synagogue (p. 100)
the gathering place where Jewish People pray and learn about God

temptation (p. 36)
an attraction to choose sin

Ten Commandments (p. 77)
the Laws of God's covenant given to Moses on Mount Sinai

theological virtues (p. 220)
faith, hope, love

venial sin (p. 36)
less serious sin that hurts a person's friendship with God

virtue (p. 149)
a good habit that helps us to act according to God's love for us

witnesses (p. 165)
people who speak and act based upon what they know and believe about Jesus

worship (p. 85)
giving God thanks and praise

Index

The following is a list of topics that appear in the pupil's text.
Boldface indicates an entire chapter or section.